RETURN TO THE UN

By the same author

ECONOMIC POWER IN ANGLO–SOUTH AFRICAN DIPLOMACY

DIPLOMACY AT THE UN (*edited with Anthony Jennings*)

INTERNATIONAL POLITICS: STATES, POWER AND CONFLICT
   SINCE 1945

THE POLITICS OF THE SOUTH AFRICA RUN: EUROPEAN
   SHIPPING AND PRETORIA

Return to the UN

UN Diplomacy in Regional Conflicts

G. R. Berridge

Department of Politics
University of Leicester

St. Martin's Press   New York

First published in the United States of America in 1991

Printed in Great Britain

ISBN 0–312–05270–7

Library of Congress Cataloging-in-Publication Data
Berridge, Geoff.
Return to the UN : UN diplomacy in regional conflicts / G.R.
Berridge.
   p. cm.
Includes index.
ISBN 0–312–05270–7
1. United Nations. 2. Pacific settlement of international
disputes. I. Title.
JX1977.B39   1991
341.5′23—dc20   90–42083
                                          CIP

For my mother and father

Contents

List of Appendices

List of Acronyms

ANC	African National Congress
ASEAN	Association of South-East Asian Nations
CGDK	Coalition Government of Democratic Kampuchea (the Khmer Rouge-dominated 'resistance coalition', nominally led by Prince Sihanouk)
DRA	Democratic Republic of Afghanistan (the Soviet-backed 'Kabul regime')
EC	European Community
Enosis	union between Greece and Cyprus
FAPLA	Forçãs Armadas Populares de Libertação de Angola
KPNLF	Khmer People's National Liberation Front
MPLA	Popular Movement for the Liberation of Angola (the Soviet/Cuban-backed movement controlling the government in Luanda)
OAU	Organisation of African Unity
PDPA	People's Democratic Party of Afghanistan (the Afghan Communist Party)
PLO	Palestine Liberation Organisation
Polisario	Frente Popular par la Liberación de Saguia el-Hamra y Rio de Oro (the Algerian-backed liberation movement in Western Sahara)
PRK	People's Republic of Kampuchea (the Vietnamese-backed 'Phnom Penh regime')
SADF	South African Defence Force
SWAPO	South-West Africa People's Organisation
TRNC	Turkish Republic of Northern Cyprus
UNAVEM	United Nations Angola Verification Mission
UNFICYP	United Nations Peace-keeping Force in Cyprus
UNIFIL	United Nations Interim Force in Lebanon
UNITA	National Union for the Total Independence of Angola (the Western-backed movement led by Jonas Savimbi)
USUN	United States Mission at the United Nations

Acknowledgements

I am grateful for the help of librarians at the University of Leicester Library, the Royal Institute of International Affairs (London), and the United Nations office in London. I am also very grateful for the helpful criticisms of portions of the manuscript made at short notice by Alan James and Maurice Keens-Soper, neither of whom is responsible for any remaining errors of fact or failings of judgement. Finally, I would like to thank my mother for assistance with the typing, and the Nuffield Foundation for a generous grant.

Leicester   GRB

Introduction

It is probable that no country is more closely associated with the United Nations than Switzerland. Despite its long tradition of neutrality, it was an original member of the League of Nations, the UN's predecessor, and provided the site of its headquarters at Geneva.[1] Geneva is now the European headquarters of the United Nations and the international headquarters for some of its major satellite organisations. Furthermore, some of the most important conferences held under UN auspices since the Second World War have been held there. Not surprisingly, the canton of Geneva earns approximately ten per cent of its income from the United Nations,[2] which spends in that city about thirty per cent of its ordinary budget.[3] Nevertheless, Switzerland itself refused to join the UN on the grounds that membership would compromise its neutrality. On 16 March 1986 the citizens of Switzerland held a referendum in order to decide if this longstanding decision should be reversed. The Federal government and both houses of parliament strongly supported the proposition that the country should become a full member, largely on the grounds that non-membership cut the country off from diplomatic discussions vital to its interests while its neutrality would not in practice be compromised since collective security was a dead letter.[4] This case was also supported almost unanimously by the Swiss press.[5] Nevertheless, on a relatively high turnout, the Swiss voted by a margin of roughly three to one to remain outside the organisation.[6] Even in Geneva itself almost 70 per cent of those who voted were against memberhip.

Of course, there were local reasons for the scale of this popular rejection of the UN. Apart from having to face the enduring strength of dogmatic neutralist sentiment, the supporters of the UN, numerically dominated as it is by Third World countries, also ran head-on into an upsurge of 'neo-Helvetic fundamentalism'[7] fed by growing anxiety over immigration from the Third World. The extreme right-wing, anti-immigrant opposition – led by Nationale Aktion in German-speaking Switzerland and Vigilance Party in French-speaking Switzerland – were also fortunate in being able to exploit a controversy at the time over an influx of Tamil refugees from Sri Lanka.[8] Nevertheless, there was also wide agreement among commentators on the Swiss political scene that another factor was the generally low esteem in which the United Nations was held in Switzerland, which merely reflected prevailing European and North American sentiment. The Swiss rejection of the UN in March 1986, in other words, was the nadir of its post-war unpopularity in the developed non-communist world. In less than a year the situation was almost entirely transformed. It was transformed, too, as a result of a much fuller exploitation of the potential of the UN to which the Swiss Foreign Ministry had repeatedly drawn attention in the referendum campaign: its diplomatic potential.

In July 1987 the Security Council passed Resolution 598 which required a cease-fire in the Gulf War. This was immediately accepted by Iraq and accepted by Iran a year later. In September the United Nations was given pride of place by Mikhail Gorbachev in the 'new thinking' in Soviet foreign policy. In April 1988 a UN-brokered settlement of the Afghanistan crisis – probably the most serious cause of the new cold war in the first half of the 1980s – was signed. In September the UN's peacekeeping forces were awarded the Nobel Peace Prize. And in December 1988 a settlement in Angola/Namibia, to which the United Nations had contributed more significantly than is usually acknowledged (especially in the United States) was sealed in New York.

The UN's main contribution to 'peace-making' has thus been made where it is most needed: in those conflicts which, since the diplomatic lexicon inevitably reflects the perspective of the superpowers, are known as 'regional conflicts'. As Sir Anthony Parsons has pointed out, it is not where NATO and the Warsaw Pact face each other directly, in Europe, but 'in other areas, particularly the Middle East, where the perceived "vital interests" of both superpowers are engaged but the ground rules are not clear and the policies of the regional states are not under control, that the real danger lies'.[9]

Why do states turn to the United Nations and why have they been turning to it with almost unprecedented enthusiasm since 1987? What has been the nature of the UN contribution to the settlements mentioned above, and what contribution is it making to extant problems such as those in the Western Sahara, Cyprus and Kampuchea? Does it have any relevance to what, despite the Egypt–Israel peace treaty, may still be the most serious of all 'regional conflicts', that between the Arabs and the Israelis? These are the main questions addressed in this book.

Part I
Changes at Headquarters

1 The Security Council and 'Secret Diplomacy'

The Security Council is the most important organ of the United Nations and, in the words of the Charter (see Appendix 1), is charged with 'primary responsibility for the maintenance of international peace and security'. It has fifteen members: five permanent and veto wielding ones (the United States, the Soviet Union, Britain, France and the People's Republic of China); and ten elected for two-year terms in the light of the need for 'equitable geographical distribution' (see Appendix 3). The presidency of the Council rotates on a monthly basis among both permanent and non-permanent members. In contrast to the first two decades of its existence, when it was dominated by the Western powers, no group of states now holds sway over the Security Council – lest it be 'the Big Five' themselves.

INSTITUTIONALISING 'INFORMAL CONSULTATIONS'

An important contribution to the ease with which the Security Council slipped into the role of top-level forum for negotiations between the big powers in recent crises is to be found in the way in which it has responded to calls for procedural innovation over the last few decades: it has resisted the bad ones and adopted the good. The major bad suggestion which it resisted was for a further enlargement of its membership after that adopted in 1965 (see page 5. Any additional increase in size would almost certainly have made it too unwieldy for diplomacy (though this is not to say that changes in the *nature* of its membership might not have been, and remain, advisable).[1] The most important of the good suggestions which it accepted was for the institutionalisation of 'informal consultations'.

Instead of meeting only in public and thus inevitably being little more than a platform for hostile exchanges in the East–West propaganda war, as was generally the case before, the practice developed of holding informal private meetings of the Security Council and extensive 'informal consultations' among its members in which the president for the month invariably played a focal role. These practices did not replace the public meetings, of course, but

3

increasingly made them rubber-stamping affairs in which often neither debates nor votes on a consensus achieved in private were required. When did they develop? Why did they develop? What was their significance? And why were there mixed feelings about them in the Secretariat and elsewhere?

From the beginning, rules of procedure agreed by the Security Council at its first meetings in early 1946 had provided for private meetings – to the outrage of some small and medium member states[2] – and stipulated that deliberations on the appointment of a secretary-general should always be held in closed session.[3] (The 'provisional' rules of procedure of the Security Council, as amended in 1982, are reproduced in full in Appendix 2.) It also became customary for the Security Council to meet in private to discuss the draft Annual Report prepared in the Secretariat.[4] However, these were *formal* private meetings, governed by the rules of procedure, and while three *informal* private meetings were held during the Suez crisis in October 1956,[5] it seems that it was not until the late 1960s or early 1970s that the Council began regularly to hold private discussions of this kind when dealing with substantive matters of international peace and security.[6]

From the account of Lord Caradon, who was Britain's widely respected Ambassador at the UN from 1964 until 1970, what seems to have happened is that the move away from reliance on confrontational public meetings of the Council began with informal consultations, and then 'developed still further'. Writing in 1985, he said: 'Now there is what amounts to a Security Council in private, where all the members, together with the president of the council and the secretary-general, meet in a separate, and specially provided, room with full interpretation facilities . . .'[7] (Construction of this special room, close to the public Security Council chamber, was completed in 1978.)[8] Drawing on the language of the British parliamentary tradition, these meetings came to be referred to within the UN as 'informal consultations of the whole'.[9]

Inevitably, there was some confusion during the evolution of the informal private meeting: it was sometimes not obvious, even to its members, what kind of a meeting the Council was holding.[10] During the 1970s, however, the distinction between a formal and an informal private meeting became clearly established, and was not likely to be misunderstood once the special room was completed since formal closed meetings take place in the main Security Council Chamber. Unlike these, then, informal sessions are not preceded by the circulation of an agenda, no record of discussions of any kind is kept, the Secretary-General is not required to issue a communiqué at their conclusion, and – ultimate sign of informality – they are given no number by the Secretariat. In short, informal private meetings of the Security Council do not officially exist![11]

The most important reason for the development of informal consultations and closed sessions of the Security Council in the second half of the 1960s, in a word, *secrecy*, was that the Council members needed, for the first time, to engage in genuine diplomacy on a broad and continuing inter-caucus basis. And the reason that they needed to engage in this kind of diplomacy was the same reason that usually produces diplomacy in the end – the development of a balance of power. In 1965, under pressure from the Non-Aligned Movement, the Security Council, which since its inception had contained eleven members, was increased to fifteen by the addition of four more non-permanent members. The West had lost its dominance but had not been replaced by another all-powerful group of states. In the enlarged Council, as one of the UN's own procedural experts has commented, 'it is difficult, if not impossible, for any power or group to force a decision of importance. Any substantive decision or consensus', he concludes, 'can be achieved only through consultation, negotiation, and compromise . . .'.[12]

It is also likely that the Security Council has retreated more and more into informal consultations as a result of the growing tendency of non-members to demand – and receive – a hearing at public Council debates when their interests are deemed to be involved. Beginning in 1971, this included liberation movements as well as states, and it was not long after that, as Sydney Bailey has noted, that 'the Council was inviting anyone whom the majority of members wished to hear'.[13] 'Visiting firemen', as they are ironically known in New York,[14] were especially attracted to the Namibia debates. In 1983 there were sixty-three and in 1985 fifty-nine.[15] Sir Colin Crowe, the career diplomat appointed as Britain's UN Ambassador in 1970 by the new Conservative government, was not speaking only for himself when in 1977 he wearily observed that 'too many countries with only marginal interest in the question at issue take up the time and the physical stamina of the Council without contributing anything to the debate, often downgrading it by irrelevancies or invective'.[16]

Further fillips to the process of informal consultation were given by external developments. In November 1968 an American government was elected which had some inclination to acknowledge strategic parity with the Soviet Union and talk the language of the balance of power. In 1971 the communist government in Peking was installed in China's permanent seat on the Security Council in place of the American client regime on Taiwan. A marked improvement in US–Soviet and US–Chinese relations took place at roughly the same time. And in 1967 and 1973 acute crises erupted in the Middle East which served to remind the members of the Security Council of the implications of their *common interest* in the avoidance of nuclear war.

THE DARK SIDE OF SECRECY?

Wilsonianism ('Open covenants, *openly arrived at*') is fortunately now out of fashion and as a result the case for 'secret diplomacy' (like 'formal treaty', a pleonasm) rarely has to be restated for the benefit of governments.[17] Since the members of the Security Council are clearly required by the Charter to engage in diplomacy among themselves, it would thus seem unlikely that there would be any significant opposition to the development of informal consultations and closed sessions. There is also wide testimony that these procedures had proved their worth long before the current re-birth of enthusiasm for genuine UN diplomacy: in making possible direct negotiations in certain crises, such as those which produced the guidelines for a peace settlement during the Middle East crisis of 1967;[18] and in facilitating the negotiation of resolutions which sanctify agreements achieved in diplomacy conducted elsewhere, as following the Yom Kippur War in 1973.[19]

Such successes were assisted not only by the lesser pressure for posturing and reduced vulnerability to sabotage made possible by secrecy but also by the limited collegiality which developed among representatives of otherwise unfriendly powers in these circumstances. Lord Caradon, himself a very collegial person and well known in the British Foreign Office for his inclination to put the UN interest before what they took to be the British,[20] emphasises this but he is not alone.[21] Nevertheless, serious reservations have been expressed about the development of informal discussions and informal private meetings of the Security Council. What are they? Where do they come from? What are they worth?

Oddly enough, the UN Secretariat itself has been a major source of unease about the flourishing process of informal consultation. Odd, because civil servants are supposed to have a reflexive preference for anonymity and also because it might be imagined that the torch-bearers of the UN idea would be enthusiastic about anything that oiled the engine of their machine. Perhaps the unease has been encouraged by the fear of the Secretariat, seeing itself since the time of Hammarskjöld as a lobby for the rights of the smaller states, that secrecy will make the Security Council seem even more the preserve of the big powers, especially since this development has coincided with a refusal of the permanent members to contemplate its further enlargement. Perhaps, too, it is fuelled by the fact that in private the Council's delegates tend to be more critical of past failures of UN organs![22]

Kurt Waldheim, who was elected Secretary-General at the end of 1970 and held the position throughout the period when informal consultation was institutionalised, was himself a critic of the procedure. In a statement that he made to a seminar on the Security Council in November 1977, Waldheim observed that it would be harmful if it appeared that the Council 'were simply rubber-stamping agreements that had been reached in secret behind the scenes'. In explanation of this claim, the Secretary-General added that 'A minimum of discussion and debate in formal meetings is essential to enable the public and the media to *understand* not only the full significance of any action authorised by the Council but also to *understand* the essentials of how any consensus is achieved' (emphasis added).[23] In short, Waldheim's view was that informal consultations were in danger of robbing the Security Council of its *educational* function.

This argument is not immediately convincing. Moreover, Waldheim, as his close colleague Brian Urquhart has since observed, was an 'energetic, ambitious mediocrity',[24] who was in fact obsessed with publicity. This was not altogether unconnected to his feverish campaigns for re-election, first in 1976 and then – unsuccessfully – in 1981. According to Urquhart, 'the public image rather than the substance of a question tended to be the reality in his mind'.[25] Clearly, Waldheim felt that if the Security Council hid its light too much under a bushel the UN's reputation would suffer – and so would his own. Indeed, he constantly lamented the fact that the Security Council did not get the credit it deserved for contributing to the settlement, or containment, of dangerous international problems.[26]

Having said all this, Waldheim's point of view should not be dismissed on *ad hominem* grounds. The UN's stock in the 1970s was very low and in the United States, where it counted most, was getting lower. It is also perfectly true, as he said in his annual report in September 1979, that 'The capacity of an organisation to deal effectively with its business and *to be seen to have a useful impact* is an essential basis for public confidence' (emphasis added).[27] Perhaps in arguing for a balance between private business and public theatre in the Security Council he had got it right. Waldheim is also supported by an interesting section in Andrew Boyd's outstanding history of the Security Council where he deals with the aftermath of the 1967 war in the Middle East. Having described how the official record of the Council's proceedings on 8 and 9 July emphatically gave the lie to an important thrust of pro-Israeli propaganda at that time (that U Thant had surrendered to Russian and Arab pressure in agreeing to put UN observers on the Suez Canal), Boyd observes that 'The public nature of so much of the Council's activity may sometimes impair its effectiveness, but there are times, like this one, when it is good that the truth is made easy for all to see . . .'[28]

A much less persuasive objection to informal consultations comes from Waldheim's critic, Brian Urquhart himself. While agreeing, in an article published in 1981, that the Security Council 'is a more cautious, less dramatic body than it was . . . an experienced body of highly competent and responsible professionals, accustomed to working with each other and to discussing serious matters in a constructive and non-polemical way . . .', and implicitly attributing this to the development of informal consultations and informal private meetings, he is more concerned to advance a warning about the dark side of this change in procedure. This is that 'the consultation process' is a useful pretext for avoiding public meetings of the Security Council when no consensus can be achieved, and that in consequence the Secretary-General, upon whom the burden of dealing with international crises is thus placed more and more, is deprived of the 'strong and consistent backing necessary for his effectiveness'. In short, informal consultations contain the danger of encouraging 'an increasingly expedient and evasive approach to world problems' on the part of the Security Council, and this in turn 'does little to increase its prestige or the public respect in which it should be held.'[29] In the following year, this disquiet also surfaced in the 'Report of the Secretary-General on the work of the Organisation', which is not surprising since it was drafted by Urquhart.[30] Having noted that 'In recent years the Security Council has increasingly resorted to the valuable process of informal consultations', Javier Pérez de Cuéllar immediately added that 'there is sometimes a risk that this process may become a substitute for action by the Security Council or even an excuse for inaction'.[31]

This argument has four problems. In the first place, Urquhart implies that public meetings of the Security Council were more or less inescapable before the full-scale development of informal consultation, though the history of the Council does not support this. A classic example of Security Council torpidity in the earlier period occurred on the eve of the Six-Day War in 1967.[32] In the second place, Urquhart seems to assume (the argument here is not very clearly advanced) that public debate within a divided Council is more likely to foster agreed approaches to 'world problems', though why this should be so is by no means self-evident. Why should national delegates (by virtue of the public setting, perforce addressing mainly national audiences) be able to achieve a consensus in public which they cannot achieve in private? Besides, as Davidson Nichol shrewdly observes, while a public failure by the Security Council to reach agreement as a result of a veto 'blocks a certain line of approach' for some time, 'a decision by the Council informally to do nothing for the time being leaves options open'.[33] In the third place, while it is true that unproductive 'mumbling behind closed doors', to borrow Urquhart's phrase, may do little to increase the prestige of the Security Council, it is also hard to see how this might be increased by bellowing through open ones. On the contrary, as Sir Colin Crowe points out, it is the 'impression of a united Council' created by the premium placed on the search for consensus which has 'a much greater impact on public opinion'.[34] And in the fourth place, the argument suggests that Security Council resolutions necessarily are, or necessarily engender, 'action', when historically this has commonly not been the case.

If the Security Council cannot reach agreement in private, no diplomatic (as opposed to propaganda) point is served by airing its disagreements in public. This will only entrench positions more deeply, poison the atmosphere further and advertise its inability to act at least as eloquently as failing to meet publicly at all.

PRE-EMPTIVE DISCUSSION AND 'PERIODIC' MEETINGS

While the Security Council was well adjusted to meet the crises of 1987–9 by virtue of its still relatively small membership and institutionalised process of informal consultation, there were two regards in which some believed it still to be procedurally retarded. It had failed to institute pre-emptive meetings, and it had failed to introduce a system of regular meetings at the 'summit' or at least at foreign minister level. However, the seriousness of the first omission was probably exaggerated, while the history of the second suggested some hope for the future.

In his Annual Report for 1982, pre-emptive discussions by the Security Council were the first suggestion made by the Secretary-General for a strengthening of the UN's peace-making machinery. 'If the Council were to keep an active watch on dangerous situations and, if necessary, initiate discussions with the parties *before* they reach the point of crisis,' said de Cuéllar, 'it might often be possible to defuse them at an early stage before they degenerate into violence' (emphasis added).[35] In Britain this call was supported most notably by Sir Anthony Parsons, who came to public attention as Britain's permanent representative at the UN during the Falklands crisis in 1982, and was subsequently appointed Foreign Affairs Adviser to Mrs Thatcher.[36] Both appear to have had in mind the failure of the Council to anticipate either the outbreak of fighting in the Gulf in 1980 or the invasion of Lebanon by Israel in 1982, despite the fact that the inevitability of these events was obvious some time before they occurred. Of course, as Sir Anthony Parsons knows, this innovation will require the exercise of more initiative in calling meetings by the Secretary-General himself, since the Council only fails to meet in these circumstances when one or more weighty members have good reason for not calling one themselves. This will mean risking unpopularity and, as a result, the Secretary-General may have to be denied the opportunity of re-election if he is to be expected to act without reference to self-interest. Even if the corollary of such a change were a longer fixed term,[37] this would be a pity.

The UN Charter requires the Security Council to hold meetings at which, by implication, not only is the international situation discussed in a general way (without the need to focus on a specific crisis and produce any detailed decision) but at which the member states are represented at high ministerial level. These are known – not very illuminatingly – as 'periodic meetings'. However, despite the Charter obligation, despite the fact that the Security Council's own Rules of Procedure call for such horizon-gazing summit meetings to be held twice a year, despite support for them from the first four Secretaries-General, and despite several calls for them to be held by the General

Assembly, only two have ever taken place. The first occurred in October 1970, at the time of the UN's 25th Anniversary, following an initiative by Finland's permanent representative, the extremely able Max Jakobson. The second took place in 1985 as part of the celebrations of the UN's 40th Anniversary.[38]

The case for periodic meetings of the Security Council is the case for summit meetings in general, with four added points. First, freed from concern with immediate crises, they should be able to generate 'a more preventive-constructive approach to international problems'.[39] Secondly, they would help to create 'a new channel of communication between the permanent and elected members'.[40] Thirdly, they would create a better public image of the Security Council.[41] And fourthly, in contrast to most non-routine summits, 'Ministers could safely drop into the chairs around it [the Council table] once or twice a year without panicking about coming away "empty handed"'.[42] The Finnish proposal suggested that one should be held in spring and the other in autumn, the latter to coincide with the presence of foreign ministers in New York for the opening of the General Assembly. It also suggested that they should normally be closed.[43]

Unfortunately, despite the first hints of East–West detente in late 1970, there remained insufficient common ground among the permanent members to make it likely that a periodic meeting would produce anything other than set-piece speeches and banal pronouncements, and this is what happened at the first meeting. As a former president of the Council pointed out in 1977, with tactful understatement, the 'mixed membership' of the Council made it highly unlikely that ministers would use it to air 'intimate thoughts or new initiatives' even in private.[44] The sterility of the 1970 meeting was undoubtedly responsible for the failure to repeat the experiment until fifteen years later, and then the meeting, which this time was public, was largely ceremonial.[45]

Nevertheless, by 1985 the principle that periodic meetings should be held had been accepted by the Council and had been put into practice on two occasions. Moreover, while they had not been spectacular successes, they had not been spectacular failures either. Should the international climate improve, therefore, there were precedents upon which to draw. In this way, too, then, the Security Council was prepared to be – as Jakobson had hoped it would in 1970 – 'the centre for international consultations on the vital issues affecting world peace'.[46]

2 The Secretariat under Pérez de Cuéllar

If the United Nations was well prepared to seize the opportunities presented to it in 1987 by virtue of changes in Security Council procedure, it was also well prepared in having the correct man in the Secretary-General's office. Javier Pérez de Cuéllar had just the right amount of experience as well: enough to understand the possibilities and limitations of his office; not so much that he had become jaded and cynical. And in the process he had maintained 'reasonably good relations with all the main groups and blocs'.[1] Interestingly, Mrs Thatcher, not one of the UN's greatest admirers, is believed to hold him in high regard.[2]

Pérez de Cuéllar is a Peruvian of aristocratic Spanish descent. He is a law graduate of Lima's Catholic University and a career diplomat. He joined the Peruvian foreign ministry in 1940 and the diplomatic service in 1944. He had extensive tours of duty in Europe and South America, and would understand the Swiss attitude to the UN very well since he was Ambassador there from 1964 until 1966. In the second half of the 1960s he reached the top of his profession, from 1966 until 1969 acting as Permanent Under-Secretary and Secretary-General of the Foreign Office and from there going as Peru's first Ambassador to the Soviet Union, a post which he occupied until 1971.

Before becoming Secretary-General, however, Pérez de Cuéllar also had extensive experience of the United Nations on both sides of the fence. As a member of his country's delegation, he had attended the very first session of the General Assembly in 1946, and from 1971 until 1975 had been Peru's Permanent Representative in New York (for two of these years Peru was on the Security Council). He then moved over to the Secretariat, serving as Waldheim's Special Representative in Cyprus from October 1975 until December 1977 and as Under-Secretary-General for Special Political Affairs from February 1979 until May 1981, coupling this with the post of Personal Representative of the Secretary-General on the situation in Afghanistan for much of the latter year. (In the interim he had been recalled by the tottering military government in Lima to act as Ambassador to its oil-rich neighbour, Venezuela, possibly in the hope that Pérez de Cuéllar's skills would produce some backing for Peru, which was on the verge of bankruptcy.) He thus had UN experience in the field as well as at head office. His qualifications for the post were, as the United States representative said at the General Assembly meeting on 15 December 1981 when he took the oath of office, 'superb'.[3]

Pérez de Cuéllar became Secretary-General of the United Nations on 1 January 1982, the fifth in the organisation's history and the first from Latin America. He had emerged the previous autumn as the compromise candidate after the main candidates, Kurt Waldheim (seeking a third term) and Salim Salim of Tanzania were persuaded to withdraw. (Waldheim was vetoed by the Chinese and Salim by the Americans.) The Peruvian diplomat had not campaigned for the office and when the news of his election was telephoned to him at a beach house outside Lima he was 'dumbfounded'.[4] In October 1986, following a unanimous recommendation by the Security Council, Pérez de Cuéllar was reappointed for a second five-year term by acclaim in the General Assembly. There had been no other candidates for the office. Having thus been virtually drafted once more (he had initially said that he would serve only one five-year term and at the time of his reappointment was recovering from major heart surgery), election debts weighed as lightly on Pérez de Cuéllar after this election as they had after his first.[5] When the UN hit its winning streak in the following year, he was 67 years old.

There is universal agreement on the main points of Pérez de Cuéllar's personality, character, and diplomatic style. The adjective which is most often used to describe the personality and style of the present Secretary-General is the capacious word 'quiet', which means variously modest, bland, uncharismatic, contemplative,[6] selfless, softly spoken, and civilised. This quietness entails a lack of interest in his public image, which is reflected in infrequent press conferences. According to one illuminating press profile, 'he recoils from the limelight and gives an impression of acute discomfort when confronted by television'.[7] Those who know him well also say that he is highly intelligent, self-assured (but cautious as well), composed, meticulous, tenacious, and fortunately one of nature's optimists. (At the end of a lecture given at Oxford in 1986 he said that 'However grim the past and present may seem, the Secretary-General has to remain firm in his belief that . . . the movement towards good has an enduring appeal, and that good will triumph in the end'.)[8] His integrity is universally acknowledged, and in the Secretariat itself (where low morale made this important) he is admired for his extreme courtesy and consideration, as well as for his other qualities. Though Pérez de Cuéllar resembles his predecessor in diplomatic style, his other qualities set him above Waldheim. This contrast has helped him as well.

As Urquhart has pointed out, the fact that Pérez de Cuéllar has a rather bland, low-key style does not mean to say that he is without imagination. At least as far as organisational matters are concerned, moreover, he has 'no inhibitions about sticking his neck out'.[9] This outspokenness, particularly in his first annual reports, also boosted his prestige inside and outside the Secretariat, even though it was not always well directed. In September 1982, when the new Secretary-General delivered his first annual report to the General Assembly (drafted by Brian Urquhart), he departed from the usual practice of surveying the broad range of work of the UN and instead focused on 'the central problem of the Organisation's capacity to keep the peace and to serve as a forum for negotiations'. The reason for this, he said, was that current international conditions made it 'even more difficult than usual' for the UN to function properly; there was a 'crisis in the multilateral approach in international affairs'.

The 'most urgent goal', said Pérez de Cuéllar's first report, was to rejuvenate the Security Council, and he had plenty of advice for the permanent members as to how they should pursue this. In addition to stressing the need for pre-emptive diplomatic interventions and warning that informal consultations should not be allowed to become an excuse for inaction, as noted in Chapter 1, he wanted the Council's procedures to be streamlined so that it could act more 'swiftly and decisively in crises'. Next, he said that 'new ways' should be devised of organising 'concerted diplomatic action' behind the Secretary-General when he was trying to follow up a Security Council resolution. (This last point clearly came from the heart. 'There is a tendency in the United Nations', said Pérez de Cuéllar, 'for Governments to act as though the passage of a resolution absolved them from further responsibility for the subject in question . . . In fact', he continued, 'resolutions, particularly those unanimously adopted by the Security Council, should serve as a springboard for governmental support and determination and should motivate their policies outside the United Nations'. He was even more critical of the permanent members on this score in his second annual report.) In the case of peacekeeping operations, these might be stiffened by 'explicit guarantees for collective or individual supportive action'. (He seemed doubtful that peacekeeping would be improved by increasing the 'military capacity or authority' of the Blue Berets.) Finally, he said, 'the Council itself could devise more swift and responsive procedures for sending good offices missions, military or civilian observers or a United Nations presence to areas of potential conflict'. Throughout the report there was an emphasis on 'prevention' rather than cure and introducing the necessary procedures in a 'systematic' way.[10] Though he was disappointed at the subsequent failure of the Security Council to change its ways, Pérez de Cuéllar kept returning to these themes in subsequent speeches and reports.

If the new Secretary-General showed his mettle early on by critical observations on the attitude to the UN of the bigger powers *in general*, he was nevertheless careful to interpret his brief judiciously, and therefore not court the risk of giving serious offence to them individually – the fate which had befallen both Trygve Lie and the 'high and splendid' Hammarskjöld.[11] At his first press conference as Secretary-General, Pérez de Cuéllar had made clear that his 'general philosophy' of the job was 'to help solve all international problems peacefully'. He added that he was especially anxious to see Namibia independent and progress on the north–south dialogue, not least because in the long term the latter was of 'fundamental importance' to the 'solution of the problem of international peace and security' (in his earlier acceptance speech he had said in this connection that he could not separate himself from his origins in a developing country).[12] Nevertheless, he emphasised that he was not prepared to make critical comments on Security Council or General Assembly decisions or try to 'impose' his good offices in disputes.[13] In an address at the Sorbonne in Paris a few years later he said that 'the Secretary-General is not the chief executive of a world government . . . Nor is he a secular pope who can pronounce anathemas and issue edicts in the temporal realm'.[14]

What Pérez de Cuéllar *was* determined to do – and what in the years before 1987 he succeeded in doing – was to steer a course in the fulfilment of his political role between two temptations: 'the Scylla' of 'aggrandisement' and 'the Charybdis' of 'extreme caution',[15] that is to say, though he did not say this himself, between the model of Hammarskjöld and the model of Thant. In his Sorbonne address the Secretary-General said that while common prudence and the requirements of the Charter precluded him from unqualified entrance into any political fray, 'These constraints . . . do not justify a passivity on his part in regard to general turns in international relations or the responsibilities of the various parties in a particular situation. Though the exercise of his political functions can bear fruit only in a climate of reasonableness,' he continued, 'he cannot merely wait for the atmosphere to change and the tide to turn . . . his job is to look for, and take advantage of, whatever openings come to view for better communications and greater accommodation between States that are at odds with one another . . . He has to be impartial but not indifferent'. In this connection he had observed in his annual report in 1982 that pre-emptive action by the Security Council might be assisted if he were 'to play a more forthright role in bringing potentially dangerous situations to the attention of the Council' (his prerogative under Article 99). However, it is interesting that in the later Sorbonne address he cautioned that it would be unwise to insist on using this prerogative if it merely resulted in 'indecision or disagreement' in the Council. Pérez de Cuéllar had got the balance just right.

SECRETARIAT TROUBLES

The right man may have been at the helm at the beginning of 1987 and he may have been strengthened by the reputation that he had acquired for being a 'reluctant incumbent'.[16] But what of the Secretariat over which Pérez de Cuéllar presided and which would have to bear the brunt of his diplomacy? Was this not 'bloated' (a favourite word of critics), demoralised, and – mainly as a result of hostility from the Reagan administration – financially on the rack? How could it, therefore, provide Pérez de Cuéllar with the energetic and efficient support that he would need?

It is certainly true that the Secretariat was not in particularly good shape at the beginning of 1987; in fact it was plagued with problems. As Pérez de Cuéllar was the first to insist, the Secretariat remained under intense political pressure from member states in the matter of appointments, not least in the question of 'inherited posts' – an obvious menace to career development and thus to staff morale, which had been getting worse and worse.[17] Even Britain, traditionally diffident in lobbying on behalf of its own nationals, was now following a more aggressive policy.[18] The General Assembly was still making Secretariat management difficult by passing resolutions which strayed into the area of the Secretary-General's responsibility. On top of this, some governments continued to make supplementary payments to their nationals employed in the Secretariat, ostensibly to encourage qualified individuals to serve the UN but obviously compromising their loyalty.[19] And despite all the talk of the 'bloated' bureaucracy, this certainly did not extend to the Secretariat's pool of skilled mediators. As Lister has pointed out, this pool was – and remains – extremely small, which is an even more pitiful state of affairs when it is recalled that the nationality of one or other of its members sometimes makes them unacceptable to one or other of the parties to a conflict.[20] In this connection, it is also worth noting that in January 1986 Brian Urquhart, the widely respected senior Under-Secretary-General, who had served the UN for forty years and was described by the Editor of *Foreign Affairs* in 1981 as 'both voice and arm of all that most needs preserving and strengthening in the United Nations',[21] retired. This was a serious loss, mitigated only by the fact that it allowed Urquhart, freed of the restraints of office, to launch on a one-man propaganda campaign on behalf of the UN.

All of these were serious problems but even collectively they paled into insignificance in the light of the UN's financial crisis, which came to a head at precisely the juncture that the world began to return to the United Nations.

By 1985 the UN was already in serious financial difficulties. This was a result of inflated budgets, defaults and delayed payments. However, the real crisis had started in that year as a result of a long-threatened change in policy towards UN regular budget contributions by the United States,[22] which was by far the biggest contributor to the UN, paying the maximum of 25 per cent of the budget. In 1985 the US Congress, hustled by the right-wing Heritage Foundation and not exactly discouraged by the Reagan administration, had finally decided to punish the UN for the anti-Western and anti-Israel attitudes of its third-world majority, the alleged mismanagement and general profligacy of the Secretariat and most of the UN system, and the alleged unfairness of its budget assessments.[23] (It had already left UNESCO in the previous year.) First, the Kassebaum Amendment was passed, which required the administration to reduce the US contribution from 25 to 20 per cent unless weighted voting on budgetary matters (giving America much more influence) was introduced in the UN by October 1986. Secondly, the Gramm-Rudman-Hollings Deficit Reduction Act was passed, which ordered immediate, across-the-board cuts in federal spending – and thus embraced UN contributions. And there was further selective withholding as well.[24] At the beginning of 1986, the United States indicated that it would pay roughly $100m less than its assessed contributions for 1985 and 1986.[25] By the end of May, less than half of the $978m total contributions payable by all members by 1 January had been collected.[26]

The effects of these measures were soon felt in the Secretariat, and beyond. In early 1986 Pérez de Cuéllar had predicted a shortfall of up to $76m on the 1986 budget (which had been voted against the opposition of the United States and many of the other big powers), and a cumulative deficit of $275m. He was also obliged to pledge all reserves to meet deficits. As a result, the Secretary-General ordered a $30m reduction in spending and then persuaded a special session of the General Assembly in April–May to agree to most of an additional $30m package of cuts. These were needed, he said, to give short-term relief in 'the most serious financial crisis' in the UN's history. Conferences were cancelled, staff recruitment was frozen, all promotions were suspended for six months, retirement at sixty was made mandatory, travel allowances and overtime pay were reduced, and so on.[27] The UN had begun to resemble a British university. In April 1986 the *UN Chronicle* informed readers that 'because of the financial crisis with which the United Nations is currently confronted', it would in future appear only quarterly rather than monthly. And UN Information Offices around the world began to limit their opening times and restrict their services. Even the duration of the 41st regular session of the General Assembly, which opened in September 1986, was reduced from thirteen to ten weeks in order to save an estimated $1.1m.[28]

Despite the economy measures introduced during 1986, the financial crisis was not alleviated. Indeed, at the 41st session of the General Assembly Pérez de Cuéllar, who observed that during recent months the UN had been operating 'on the brink of bankruptcy', with a short-term deficit expected to exceed $390m by the end of the year, predicted that during 1987 there would be a budget shortfall of $85m. The United States, he confirmed, was paying only 50 per cent of its assessed contribution. Further economies, especially on conferences and meetings, documentation and travel were introduced. But there were genuine doubts as to whether this would be enough. On 4 December the General Assembly's Fifth Committee (Administrative and Budgetary) learned that the organisation would start the new year with a cash balance of only $10m, less than one week's requirements.[29] It clung on during 1987 but, with still no change of heart in Washington and many lesser contributors defaulting or in arrears, at the end of that year its deficit remained in excess of $350m. Unless things changed radically, forecast Pérez de Cuéllar, the UN would be insolvent by mid-1988. In desperation, he was considering private borrowing.[30]

REFORM

The Secretariat, then, was clearly in deep trouble: it was widely maligned outside the Third World and subjected to increasingly severe economies. Nevertheless, the picture was by no means one of unrelieved gloom. The deep politicisation of the Secretariat at least gave most member states a venal interest in seeing the UN survive, and Pérez de Cuéllar had succeeded in strengthening the Secretariat's ability to monitor independently potentially dangerous situations, as foreshadowed in his annual report in 1982.[31] Most importantly of all, however, the General Assembly had initiated steps to reform the UN in the direction long advocated by its critics among the larger member states.

Following a Japanese proposal at the beginning of the 40th session, in December 1985 the General Assembly decided to set up an '18-member Group of High-Level Intergovernmental Experts' in order to advise on medium-and long-term measures for the administrative and financial reform of the UN as a whole, excluding the specialised agencies. Composed with the usual regard to 'equitable geographical distribution',[32] and chaired by the Norwegian, Tom Vraalsen, the 'Group of 18', as it came to be known, held sixty-seven meetings during 1986 and in August presented its report to Pérez de Cuéllar.

Describing the UN as 'too complex, fragmented and top-heavy', the Group of 18 made seventy-one recommendations for reform. These included a fifteen per cent staff cut within three years,[33] a twenty-five per cent cut in the number of senior officials,[34] consolidation of UN departments and offices throughout the world, and significant reductions in conferences, meetings and document generation. The responsibility of the Secretary-General to resist political interference in personnel policy was supported, and it was held that he should not, as a rule, extend the service of senior officials beyond ten years. Staff salaries and perks were excessive and should be reduced. Most importantly of all, the Group of 18 argued that the UN budget was presented ready-made by the Secretariat and that member states had neither the means nor the time to make major changes; in short, there was no central organ within the system which could establish priorities and relate programmes to resources. As a result, it urged that member governments should be involved in the budgetary process from the beginning, but it could not agree on how this was to be achieved! A time-limit (generally about three years) should be set on implementation, said the expert group, and the Secretary-General should be asked to report on progress to the Assembly by 1 May 1987.[35]

It was testimony to the less anti-Western atmosphere in the General Assembly, to which the financial crisis had contributed, that the Group of 18 had produced a report of this nature in such a relatively short time. It was further testimony to the new atmosphere that, although it took a great deal of long and hard bargaining, the 41st session of the General Assembly, meeting at the end of 1986, substantially endorsed the report and even approved a reformed budget process. By providing for a more elaborate scheme of consultation inside and outside the General Assembly and strengthening the overall priority-setting role of the Committee for Programme and Coordination, where reaching decisions by *consensus* was customary,[36] the new budget process made it more likely that the influence of the largest contributors would be successfully exerted. This in turn made it more likely that in future they would no longer jib at paying their full assessments. Since this was weighted voting by another name,[37] it was not without deep misgivings that it was accepted by Third World members. (The report on this 'carefully crafted formula' by the UN correspondent of *The Times* of London was headlined: 'Top Donors seize control of UN spending from Third World majority'.)[38] Be that as it may, Pérez de Cuéllar said that he had been provided with 'a blueprint for a more efficient United Nations' and the means to 'facilitate' agreement on the programmes and budget, the absence of which had so exercised the bigger, especially Western powers. The year of 1987, he said, would be a 'year of transition'.[39]

As a result of these developments there was a reasonable prospect that the Secretariat and the UN system as a whole, would progressively get into better shape, not least because of the hope that sufficient progress had been made in reform to allow the United States to resume, in due course, its full budgetary contributions. Indeed, even before the General Assembly had endorsed the Group of 18's report, there were clear signs that the White House was now anxious to minimise the damage which US withholding had been inflicting on the UN. As *The Economist* reported on 20 September 1986, 'Today the administration is putting itself forward as the UN's best friend and blaming Congress for budget cuts'.[40]

Part II
The Superpowers and the UN

3 The Russian Embrace

The changes in diplomatic procedure which had already taken place in and around the Security Council, the 'quiet' style of Pérez de Cuéllar and the favourable impact on the West of the General Assembly's reaction to the report of the Group of 18 in autumn 1986, had already prepared the ground for a return to the UN during the next few years. Then, on 17 September 1987, something happened which was not only dramatic evidence of this but provided further stimulus to the process: Mikhail Gorbachev, General Secretary of the Soviet Communist Party since March 1985, published an article in the Moscow press spelling out, among other things, the central role which the Soviet Union wished the United Nations to play in future in a 'comprehensive system of international security'.

The general lines of Gorbachev's policy had been set forth eighteen months earlier at the trail-blazing 27th Party Congress, and in August 1986 had been laid before the General Assembly. At that stage couched in the vaguest of language, it was widely regarded as little more than 'the most recent in a long line of Soviet initiatives in the first committee pledging support to general principles already enshrined in the UN Charter', and as a result evoked little enthusiasm.[1] However, the September article was much clearer and more challenging[2] and, coming only two months after the Soviet Union had cooperated in producing the Security Council resolution which gave the first real promise of an end to the Gulf War (see Chapter 5), it was not long in receiving more attention in the West. Its appearance coincided, by design, with the opening of the 42nd session of the UN General Assembly.

In his article the imaginative and politically adroit Soviet leader argued for a sweeping resurrection of the UN. The world organisation, wrote Mr Gorbachev, should have a larger role in protecting the environment and in settling economic conflicts such as those arising over the question of Third World debt. It should also have a tribunal to investigate acts of international terrorism. It should have an expanded role in setting international human rights standards on such matters as family reunification and visa regulations. In addition, the International Court of Justice based in The Hague and the International Atomic Energy Agency should both be given more authority. What was really striking, however, about Mr Gorbachev's article and

25

the subsequent elaborations on it by Foreign Minister Eduard Shevardnadze and especially international organisations expert Vladimir Petrovsky (believed to have drafted the article[3]), was the emphasis placed on the need for the United Nations to assume a much more important role in preserving military stability.

The key elements in the new Soviet policy were that there should be 'wider use' of UN military observers and peacekeeping forces in regional conflicts; that a new UN agency should be created in order to verify compliance with arms-control agreements and 'monitor the military situation in areas of conflict'; that 'extensive use should be made of all means of a [sic] peaceful settlement of disputes', including 'good offices' and 'mediation'; and that the permanent members of the Security Council 'could become guarantors of regional security'. These objectives had certain procedural corollaries which were acknowledged in Moscow. One of these was the necessity for a more independent role for the Secretary-General,[4] and another was the need for greater flexibility in the personnel, agenda and location of meetings of the Council, a flexibility which is indeed encouraged by paragraphs 2 and 3 of Article 28 of the Charter (see Appendix 1). Thus the Council should meet at foreign minister rather than ambassador level at the beginning of regular General Assembly sessions and should not deal merely with specific conflicts but 'review the international situation and jointly look for effective ways for its improvement'. Neither should meetings of the Council be confined to New York, argued Gorbachev; they should also be held 'in areas of friction and tension' and be alternated 'among the capitals of the permanent member states' as well. Further corollaries of the new policy subsequently stressed by Moscow were a revival of the Security Council's Military Staff Committee (deadlocked since April 1947 and dormant since 1948),[5] the routine earmarking of elements of the armed forces of member states for service with the UN so that a 'UN standing army' might in effect be established, and the creation of an international institute for the training of peacekeeping forces.[6] In short, the new Soviet view, swiftly echoed in Eastern Europe,[7] was that a dramatically up-graded Security Council should assume the pivotal role in questions of international peace and security long assigned to it in the UN Charter.

Of course, none of this made any sense if the UN was still the confrontational arena which it had been for most of the post-war period. Thus Soviet policy now emphasised how much things had changed in the UN in the 1980s, with even the obstructionism of the

United States and other 'imperialist circles' beginning to decline. This point was made forcefully by Petrovsky in his report on the 40th Session of the General Assembly (1985–6).[8]

Two months after the publication of this report, Petrovsky, who had spent many years in New York, had been Head of the Department of International Organisations in the Soviet Foreign Ministry since 1979, and whose own pet project was the creation of an international organisation to prevent an arms race in space (part of the Soviet 'Star Peace' proposal),[9] was promoted to the rank of Deputy Foreign Minister.[10] This was an early indication that the new Soviet policy was not merely a propaganda exercise. A more substantial one occurred very shortly after the appearance of Gorbachev's article, when in October 1987 Moscow announced that it had paid off all arrears in regular UN contributions and was even willing to pay off the $197m which it owed on peacekeeping operations which it had long opposed.[11] It is also significant that in June 1988 the Soviet Union announced that, in strong contrast with its previous policy, in future it would allow its civil servants to engage in long-term contracts with the UN and thus become genuine international civil servants.[12] In the following September it participated in two Security Council meetings at foreign minister level.[13] And on 7 December 1988 Mr Gorbachev, in the first address to the General Assembly by a Soviet leader for 28 years, underlined Soviet determination to rely henceforward more on the UN's security role by announcing major unilateral Soviet force reductions.[14]

TRADITIONAL POLICY

The change in the Soviet attitude to the UN under Mr Gorbachev has indeed been very significant but it is important not to exaggerate it. The belief that Soviet policy *towards* the UN had previously been as persistently and uniquely obstructive as Soviet policy *expressed at* the UN ('*nyet* diplomacy'[15]) is something of a cold-war myth encouraged by American propaganda. When Mr Andrei Gromyko, Moscow's man at the UN during much of the period in question, said '*nyet*' to a resolution this obviously did not mean '*nyet*' to the UN itself. In any case, though it is true that the Soviet Union formally vetoed far more Security Council resolutions than did the United States in the period of its relative isolation, which is hardly surprising, this picture had already begun to change dramatically in the early 1970s.[16] Indeed, sensible of the popularity of the UN with the non-aligned states whose sympathy it was intent to cultivate, sensible also of its utility as a diplomatic forum and vehicle for promoting settlements of certain regional conflicts, and above all increasingly sensible of the usefulness of the UN as a platform for anti-Western propaganda, the Soviet Union had always been anxious to avoid inflicting any fatal wounds on it. This was even apparent during the acute crisis in the mid-1960s brought on by the refusal of the Soviet Union (and others) to contribute towards the costs of the UN peacekeeping operations in the Middle East and the Congo.[17] It is also important to stress in this connection that Moscow was never opposed in principle either to collective security or to 'peacekeeping' (the second-best alternative designed to interpose lightly-armed 'buffer' forces between 'antagonists' rather than wage war on an 'aggressor' on behalf of his 'victim'). What it was opposed to was paying for operations to which it objected, which is, of course, entirely consistent with the Charter provisions on the veto power of permanent members of the Security Council – which on this point is entirely consistent with the principles of power politics. 'Strict observance' of the Charter was in fact a major plank in Soviet propaganda.

If the new Soviet policy on the UN did not represent a dramatic change because the Soviet Union had never put up the principled opposition to the organisation that some have suggested, it is also important to note that some of the detailed proposals made for strengthening the organisation by Mr Gorbachev and his Foreign Ministry did not come completely out of the blue either. It has already been noted that the new policy had been heralded at the 27th Party Congress held in February–March 1986,[18] but well before this some of the 'new' ideas had surfaced in Moscow. As early as 1969, Gromyko had suggested in the General Assembly that the role of the Security Council be strengthened by higher-level representation and the calling of periodic meetings on international security questions of a more *general* nature, as provided for in Article 28 (2) of the Charter. (A meeting of this kind was held in New York on 21 October 1970.)[19] Twelve years later, Leonid Brezhnev, speaking in 1981 at the 26th Party Congress, put forward a more or less identical proposal, calling for 'a special session of the Security Council with the participation of the top leaders of its member states in order to look for keys to improving the international situation, and preventing war'.[20] Not surprisingly, the Soviet Union had supported the important move made during the 1970s to 'informal consultations' and *private* meetings of the Security Council which had begun at last to make the body the scene of serious diplomacy as well as serious propaganda.[21] Clearly, therefore, all that was new about Mr Gorbachev's procedural proposals for the Security Council was the suggestion concerning the *location* of its meetings.

Having said all this, there is no doubt that for the greater part of the post-war period the Soviet Union had resisted most efforts to strengthen the work of the UN in the security field, either by Charter revision – to which it was always bitterly opposed – or by encouraging more the energetic pursuit of existing institutions and procedures. The long years of bitter superpower rivalry which had made collective security a non-starter had left their mark. So too had the overlapping if relatively shorter period in which the Soviet Union had been 'in opposition' in the UN and thus seen nothing to gain by pursuing its own interests through the Western-dominated organisation and nothing to gain by raising its prestige in any way. Besides, since the United Nations was philosophically predicated on preserving the integrity of many states which Marxism-Leninism regarded as historically doomed, since the organisation was, in other words, a product of 'bourgeois' thought and the temple of an international system which was antagonistic to its own, the Soviet Union could hardly give it enthusiastic support and – 'peaceful coexistence' notwithstanding – at the same time remain true to its own credo.[22] Stalin himself had attached a very low priority to the UN from the beginning,[23] and the behaviour of Trygve Lie during the Korean war in the early 1950s and that of the UN's most remarkable Secretary-General, Dag Hammarskjöld, during the Congo crisis a decade later, had convinced Moscow that the organisation itself had a pro-Western bias. This left Soviet policy implacably hostile towards an activist role for the Secretary-General (including wide use of peacekeeping forces), towards a genuinely independent international civil service based on career appointees, and towards any attempt by the General Assembly to usurp the security functions of the Security Council.[24] On the eve of the announcement of the new Soviet policy, Brian Urquhart, a key officer in the Secretariat for virtually all of its life, wrote that 'The Soviet bloc had never shown any real willingness to assist in developing an active and effective international system, and in the Secretariat we had long ago learned not to expect much help or support from the Soviets'.[25] It is thus clear that what the policy statements which began with Mr Gorbachev's press article of September 1987 represented was a very strong shift in the Soviet *emphasis* on the UN's role.

THE UN IN THE 'NEW THINKING' ABOUT FOREIGN POLICY

Why did the Soviet Union adopt this new emphasis on the United Nations, a proposal for an 'activist' UN which would have made Hammarskjöld rejoice? This, of course, is a vital question because on its answer depends the durability of the new Soviet embrace of the organisation.

The short answer to this question is that a major emphasis on the United Nations is a clear corollary of the dramatically new principles of Soviet foreign policy which have come to be known as Mr Gorbachev's 'new thinking'.[26] Among these are the belief that national security is as much a political and economic as a military problem and is vitally dependent upon 'mutual security'; and that the common plight of humanity – 'interdependence' – has displaced the conflict between socialism and capitalism as the central concern of international politics. In regard to the last conclusion, the 'new thinking' draws particular attention to the Third World, where virtually all hope of a transition to socialism has been abandoned by Moscow, and where instead 'regional conflicts' are seen as locally destructive and threatening to international order. In the light of these principles, with their emphasis on common rather than conflicting interests and on the interrelatedness rather than the discreteness of problems, it is hardly surprising that Mr Gorbachev should have come out for multilateralism rather than bilateralism or regionalism: that he should have come out for 'international cooperation' of the broadest kind, rather than keeping things 'in the family . . . within the Sevens, the Five, and the like'.[27] From these beliefs it is, of course, only the shortest of steps to the conclusion that the United Nations itself must be at the centre of the 'comprehensive system of international security'.

The Soviet view appears to be that only the UN has the appropriate combination of characteristics for this role: near-universal membership, 'experience of streamlining international cooperation', and treaty-dictated pre-eminence in all matters bearing on international peace and security.[28] It is for these reasons that the UN – 'a unique international centre'[29] – is the best *forum* in which to discuss the solution of de-stabilising global problems, such as Third World debt, and the best *agency* for conducting conflict mediation, peacekeeping and related activities, especially in regional conflicts.

Of course, unreconstructed cold warriors believe that all of this is merely a propaganda exercise designed to win favour in the Third World and divide Western groupings, and was timed to exploit anger at the hostility towards the UN of the Reagan administration. However, while it would be surprising if there were not an element of this in it, there is impressive support among Soviet foreign policy specialists that the 'new thinking' is genuine and that the Russians really do want the UN to play a greater role for the reasons they give.

There is no doubt that prolonged and costly embroilment in a series of intractable regional conflicts, together with the launching of the Star Wars programme in the United States, had engendered in Moscow a realisation of the limits of its military power and diplomatic influence comparable to that which seized the first Nixon administration during the Vietnam War. Brezhnev's policy of building security on military power had failed and was seen to have failed.[30] Moscow was also obviously alarmed by the recent tendency of the United States to resort to the unilateral use of force in dangerous situations – in Libya, the Gulf and Lebanon. And on top of all this Mr Gorbachev was being driven by the increasingly urgent need to concentrate on *perestroika*. Against this background, the potential of the UN to find 'face-saving ways to get out of foreign quick-sands'[31] and at the same time, via a rejuvenated Security Council, to put a curb on American adventurism, was irresistible. It is probably also true, as Rosemary Righter argues, that Moscow was anxious to coax the United States back into full support for the organisation in order to relieve increasing pressure from the Third World for the Soviet Union to make up the short-fall in UN development programmes caused by the cessation of US payments.[32] In the light of these considerations, it seems reasonable to conclude that the Soviet embrace is firm and that it will not be transient.

THE WESTERN REACTION

Since the UN is based on essentially Western principles, it might have been imagined that the Western powers would have welcomed the Russian espousal of the organisation. However, it is clear that this was not entirely the case and that there remain deep misgivings about it in NATO capitals.

One fear is that many of the practical Soviet proposals for rejuvenating the UN will involve a great increase in bureaucracy and expenditure, and are thus inconsistent with the Group of 18's calls for retrenchment which Moscow itself has endorsed. Western diplomats also complain that Moscow is ' "spinning off ideas like a Catherine wheel" ' but failing to follow them through.[33] And there is resentment at Mr Gorbachev's attempt to cast himself as the senior statesman at the United Nations. But what is probably feeding these reactions is the deep suspicion of conservative circles in the West that the 'new thinking', of which the new Soviet UN policy is only one part, represents merely a tactical rather than a strategic shift in Soviet policy; that, in other words, Moscow's long-term objectives under Gorbachev remain as expansionist as they were under Brezhnev – or, indeed, under Lenin.

Writing after the appearance of Gorbachev's famous article of 17 September 1987, the London *Economist* said that 'So far . . . Soviet actions have suggested a wish to discomfort the Americans rather than a real eagerness to strengthen the United Nations'.[34] A year later it cautioned against making the 'mistake' of the 1970s, when concessions were made in order to boost the 'doves' in the Kremlin only to find them 'pocketing Western concessions and then turning their suddenly undovish attention to southern Africa, Ethiopia and eventually Afghanistan'.[35] This sort of reflection was also common in the United States,[36] and not unknown in other Western capitals.[37] In the light of these thoughts it is not surprising that Gorbachev's new UN policy should have produced a cautious reaction. After all, it promises a greater involvement in the working of the UN by a cleverer and more decisive Soviet government than has ever been seen before and thus an increase in Soviet influence within the organisation. Soviet proposals to revive the Military Staff Committee and create a UN standing army, for example, might give the Soviet Union a veto over the day-to-day running of peacekeeping operations, in relation to which the Secretary-General presently has considerable autonomy. Even in late 1988 most of the Western states repeatedly abstained or voted against Soviet proposals on international security in the General Assembly.[38]

Nevertheless, it would be a mistake to suggest that the Western reaction was uniformly cool, or that the response of key Western states to each part of 'new thinking' on the UN was cool. It is probably true, for example, that Britain was more willing than the United States to support the Soviet view on the rejuvenation of the Security Council as a forum for the negotiation of settlements to regional conflicts. Sir Geoffrey Howe, Mrs Thatcher's Foreign Secretary until the 1989 reshuffle, certainly expressed no reservations about Moscow's line in this regard, claiming indeed that it 'lent welcome support to our long-standing conviction that the Five can and should play a more active role'.[39] And in April 1988 Soviet commentators were already emphasising that, while the United States – 'obsessed with the old logic of confrontation' – had repeatedly refused to support Soviet proposals for a comprehensive system of international security at the 42nd session of the General Assembly, there were signs that Western opposition was crumbling. West Germany, Denmark, Greece, Canada, Spain and Australia were singled out for 'displaying interest for the new Soviet proposals'. The Soviet Union also took comfort from the fact that influential sections of the American press were also urging the administration to respond more positively.[40] And it is to the American attitude that we now turn.

4 The American Reprieve

Hostility to the UN in the United States had begun to mount in the 1960s, when America lost its automatic majority in the organisation, and had come to a predictable head during the presidency of Ronald Reagan. Contemptuous of the gap between the organisation's pretensions and its performance and resentful of the anti-Western sentiments which were so often heard in it, the attitude of the Reagan administration to the UN fluctuated between thinly concealed indifference and vitriolic dislike. (Though the lead in the anti-UN campaign was taken by the Republicans, the Democrats were not far behind.[1]) This attitude was personified by the hard-edged, hectoring, right-wing ideologue who was sent to the UN by President Reagan as his ambassador in 1981: Jeane J. Kirkpatrick, an academic specialist in Latin America.[2] The budgetary consequences for the UN of the influential Jeane Kirkpatrick, who thought that on political and security matters the UN's significance lay in the sphere of propaganda rather than diplomacy, have already been described in Chapter 2. However, as intimated at the end of that chapter, in late 1986 and early 1987 there were unmistakable signs that the White House, the State Department and the 'USUN' mission in New York, if not Congress, were mellowing towards the UN and that, as a result, a financial reprieve might be in sight. What were the reasons for this?

THE FEAR OF LOSING THE UN

Despite the anti-UN rhetoric of the Reagan administration, there is reason to believe that it contained some subterranean sympathy for the belief that even in the peace and security field the organisation retained a *potential* to be of surprising value – and that, as a result, it would be unwise to push it over the edge by starving it of US funds. Following the vital role played by the UN in the aftermath of the Yom Kippur War in October 1973, the earlier Republican administration of Richard Nixon, which had also initially been dismissive of the organisation, had arrived at the same conclusion.[3] During a speech in January 1982, Jeane Kirkpatrick herself had acknowledged the past peacemaking and peacekeeping successes of the UN and also

34

admitted that 'It has more recently played a positive role in Cyprus and Lebanon'.[4] Apart from exploiting the UN for propaganda purposes, it had also been part of her stated policy to reinforce this 'constructive' side of the UN, and as a result she had participated actively – though admittedly somewhat sceptically – in the informal meetings held by the Security Council to discuss the reforms proposed by Pérez de Cuéllar in his 1982 report.[5] Nor had President Reagan been wholly dismissive of the UN, even during 1985. While stressing the organisation's failure 'to deal effectively with essential security issues', he nevertheless repeatedly acknowledged that it 'can be a force for great good' in its 'peacekeeping and peacemaking efforts' and that for this as well as other reasons the United States continued to take the UN seriously.[6]

It is true, of course, that the Reagan administration was well schooled in the earlier arguments of right-wing critics of the UN who had argued that while the UN might periodically contribute to the resolution of serious conflicts, the fact was that in many cases – notably in the Middle East and southern Africa – it exacerbated them as well. On this argument, in other words, the UN was also 'a dangerous place'. Worse still, on balance it did more harm than good.[7] Nevertheless, by late 1986, not least because of the more combative approach to its opponents adopted by the USUN mission (though this was by no means the only reason), the atmosphere in the General Assembly had unmistakably changed. The new 'mood of accommodation on many significant issues' was first noted in the 39th session in autumn 1984,[8] and in March the following year Jeane Kirkpatrick claimed that 'the character of the debate and the resolutions is a good deal more constructive than it was, and much less abusive than it was'.[9] It was only in 1986, however, at the General Assembly's Special Session on Africa, where self-criticism was more in evidence than attacks on 'imperialism', that it was apparent that the change in atmosphere was deep-rooted and likely to endure.[10] In the new circumstances, therefore, it was clearly much more difficult for conservative critics of the UN in Washington to sustain the argument that, in the sphere of diplomacy, *on balance* the UN any longer did more harm than good. The argument was even less tenable in light of the disastrous consequences of the American attempt to employ a 'multinational' rather than UN peacekeeping force in Beirut in 1982–3 (MNF II) and Washington's increasing need to lean on the mediation of the UN in the Cyprus dispute, so threatening to NATO's southern flank.

ALLIED PRESSURE

If Washington retained a modicum of usually well-concealed respect for the diplomatic value of the United Nations, this was even more true of its friends and allies, notably in Western Europe, Canada and Japan. Most significantly, the European Community (EC), markedly less under the thumb of Israel than was the United States, was inclined to see an international conference under UN auspices as the only hope in the Arab-Israeli dispute. Speaking on behalf of the twelve members of the EC in the General Assembly's plenary debate on the Group of 18 report on 14 October 1986 (Britain held the EC Presidency during the second half of 1986), the British permanent representative, Sir John Thomson, said that 'The Twelve wish at the outset to reaffirm their support for the Charter and for the Organisation. A world like ours,' he continued, 'whose nations are increasingly interdependent, has a correspondingly greater need for strong and vital multilateral institutions. The United Nations itself is the cornerstone of the multilateral system.'[11] Two days later the EC restated its firm belief in the value of UN peacekeeping in the General Assembly's Special Committee on Peace-Keeping.[12] Canada, of course, had a long and honourable identification with UN diplomacy going back to Lester Pearson,[13] while the Japanese had a special reason for opposing the American line. Since the early 1970s they had aspired to have their 'economic superpower' status confirmed by admission as the sixth permanent member of the Security Council.[14] (Japan is the second largest individual contributor to the UN's regular budget after the United States.) This presupposed a viable United Nations.

While sharing many of America's critical attitudes to the United Nations, therefore, Washington's allies had never supported the policy of withholding contributions to the regular budget in order to forward the process of reform, and as the UN's financial crisis worsened during 1986 so their anxiety at its implications mounted. Already paying almost thirty per cent of the regular budget (and thus collectively already an even bigger contributor than the United States), the EC states were also moved by the unappetising prospect of being forced to pick up the bill which the United States was now refusing to pay. This also included the separate funding of peacekeeping operations.[15]

In March 1986 three EC ambassadors, having failed to gain access directly to US Secretary of State, George Shultz, informed him in correspondence that America was in danger of violating its treaty obligations by cutting its UN contributions and warned him that the EC would not increase its share in order to compensate for their loss.[16] In May, the division within the Western alliance on this subject was made even plainer at the Resumed 40th Session of the General Assembly called by Pérez de Cuéllar to discuss the financial crisis. The Americans as well as the Russians were now in breach of their treaty obligations to the UN, said Sir John Thomson, and were setting a poor example to the rest of the world.[17] Pressure on Washington from its allies to pay its UN dues in full was no doubt maintained thereafter, and perhaps became marginally more effective after the Netherlands passed on the EC Presidency to Britain in July 1986. Mrs Thatcher was after all highly regarded in Washington, and Pérez de Cuéllar was in her good graces. The British government had praised his handling of the Falklands dispute, not least his decision not to bring public pressure to bear on Britain to re-open negotiations on the sovereignty issue, as mandated by the General Assembly.[18]

THE PROPAGANDA DEBIT

Budgetary withholdings from the UN's regular budget not only created another small fissure in the Western alliance but were also a handicap to American diplomacy in the Third World, where this was easily presented by Washington's enemies as symptomatic of a determination to destroy the UN altogether. This was not especially serious while the United States was in the company of other debtors (there had been plenty of these in the past) but it became more so as their ranks began to thin in the face of the mounting urgency of the UN's financial crisis and repeated appeals for full and prompt payment of assessed contributions from the Secretary-General. As 1986 progressed the United States became more and more isolated and increasingly held to blame – even by the American press – for the parlous condition of the world organisation.

Some substantial contributors in good standing with the UN, such as Canada, Britain, the Nordic countries and Australia,[19] had already promised prompter payment of their future contributions at the Resumed 40th Session of the General Assembly in April–May. But the pressure on the United States really began to mount when the other major defaulters began to break ranks. In September China notified the UN that it was paying nearly $4.4m in dues withheld over the years for various political reasons,[20] and to general surprise in the same month the Soviet Union offered a contribution of $18m to the costs of the UN peacekeeping force in Lebanon (UNIFIL).[21] (It was to be another year before Moscow announced that it had paid off all arrears on regular contributions and was even going to pay off its enormous peacekeeping debts, but – in the light of the 27th Party Congress – this was a clear harbinger of things to come.) In early December it was also reported that France, which had been in arrears to the tune of $4.35m in March, was to help out in the UN's financial crisis by paying its next full assessed contribution at the beginning of 1986.[22]

THE SUCCESS OF 'SHOCK TACTICS'

Fear of losing the UN, allied pressure and the propaganda debit were all no doubt of some significance in explaining the first signs of the American financial reprieve for the UN which were evident in the later months of 1986. There is little doubt, however, that the main reason is the obvious one: the 'shock tactics' of withholding US contributions had started to work.[23] Under the lash of poverty, UN reform was under way and Washington could not persist in its current line without flagrantly contradicting the premises on which its policy was based. What would have made this even more difficult for the administration was that during the long and difficult General Assembly deliberations over the Group of 18 report, President Reagan had intervened with personal letters to several African leaders. In these he had reaffirmed his desire to preserve the UN's credibility and clearly intimated that he would repay their support for reform by a campaign to defuse Congressional hostility to the organisation.[24]

Signs of a desire in the US administration to restrain the enthusiasm with which Congress was cutting UN budget contributions had already appeared before the start of the 41st Session of the General Assembly. But it is no accident that these became much more obvious at the conclusion of the session in December, after the General Assembly had endorsed the Group of 18 report and agreed to a budget reform which gave the big contributors much more influence. President Reagan called the reform resolution of 19 December 'historic', and Alan Keyes, the hardline Assistant Secretary of State for International Organisation Affairs, publicly claimed that the 41st session had been a 'major success' for the policies of the

Reagan administration. 'One sees', he said, 'a steady progress towards the goals that we had defined as necessary for the improvement of the United Nations'.[25] And General Vernon Walters, who had replaced Jeane Kirkpatrick as American permanent representative at the UN in May 1985, said after the key resolution was adopted that this was 'a great day for the United States . . . great for the United Nations, a great day for mankind'. He added that he would recommend 'that the United States meet its assessed contribution',[26] and in the following February he said that as a result of reforms undertaken by the UN, the administration 'is going to request from the Congress the full $209m assessment of the United States'. In addition, he said, it would also 'acknowledge the debt for what was not paid last year, and we will make arrangements to pay it off'.[27] Subsequently making this appeal to Congress, he said 'We cannot continue to neglect our financial commitments to the UN and then expect that our opinions, policies and positions will carry their former weight in the world body'.[28] In March the State Department followed this up by inviting Congress to modify the Kassebaum Amendment by accepting that 'with the adoption of General Assembly Resolution 41/213, the United Nations has taken a first concrete step toward fundamental reform on its decision-making procedures on program budget matters'; and that, in consequence, the President should be given discretion to authorise payments of assessments in excess of twenty per cent *provided* that the reforms were actually carried out.[29] The new warmth for the UN in the administration was probably also influenced by the growing reputation in the West of the Secretary-General. Even Jeane Kirkpatrick thought that he was 'a man of great intelligence, high integrity; he is', she said, 'an unusually fair, reasonable, decent man'.[30]

Paradoxically, it might have been better for the UN had Jeane Kirkpatrick still been in New York when the administration was in a position to claim the first major success for its UN policies. Her views were influential in Republican circles. By contrast, Walters, though Deputy Director of the CIA under Nixon and an enormously experienced and valued ambassador-at-large for President Reagan, was an 'implementer' rather than a maker of foreign policy.[31] He was also less confrontational in style than Kirkpatrick, personally better fitted to a diplomatic role, and – despite absences from New York on special missions for the President – had taken trouble to repair relations with other delegations at UN headquarters.[32] In short, there were probably those in Congress, where feelings were strong that the

UN reforms had not gone far enough and suspicion was deep that those promised would not materialise, who thought that Walters had gone native.

Nevertheless, at the beginning of 1987 it seemed that, although Congress would take an awful lot of turning round, there was clearly hope of an American reprieve for the UN. In the event, this proved to be much longer in coming than optimists had imagined – but the hope was there. This made it more likely that the UN would meet the challenges of the coming year in the right spirit. Moreover, the organisation was basking in new Soviet approval, reform was under way, the Security Council's habit of informal consultations was by now firmly institutionalised, and the UN was headed by a Secretary-General with the right credentials for the job; also, he was beginning his second term without election debts. The financial crisis which had dogged the UN for the last few years, and which had dominated media attention paid to it, masked the fact that in some ways it was well prepared to exploit the diplomatic opportunities of the coming months.

But no amount of spring-cleaning and diplomatic fine-tuning at the UN would have been of any avail in the absence of a marked improvement in relations between the superpowers, especially in regard to their attitude towards regional conflicts. This is why it was so important that in October 1985, speaking before the General Assembly, President Reagan had committed himself to seeking a 'fresh start' in relations with Moscow and challenged it to cooperate with Washington in trying to bring regional conflicts to an end. They should jointly urge the warring parties to negotiate; they should consult on how to reinforce or complement existing peacemaking efforts; they should perhaps offer guarantees or jointly endorse the withdrawal of foreign troops and limits on the inflow of arms; and finally, the President said, they should assist with economic rehabilitation once peace was achieved.[33] Though few would have believed it possible then, this is, more or less, what happened.

Part III
Breakthroughs in the Field

5 The Gulf War Ceasefire

On 20 July 1987 the Security Council passed resolution 598, the core of which was a *demand* that Iran and Iraq should observe immediately a comprehensive ceasefire in the fighting which had been going on between them for the last seven years and also 'withdraw all forces to the internationally-recognised boundaries without delay'. Other operative parts of the resolution provided for UN verification and supervision of the action required, repatriation of prisoners of war, the possibility of impartial inquiry into responsibility for the war, and recognition of the need for international assistance in reconstruction. It also called on the parties to cooperate in mediation efforts to proceed to a comprehensive political settlement (see Appendix 4).

Resolution 598 was passed under the most magisterial chapter of the UN Charter, Chapter VII, in the terms of which 'threats to the peace, breaches of the peace, and acts of aggression' may be extinguished by sanctions or even war. It was, in other words, a *mandatory* resolution, and it was immediately accepted by Iraq. Almost exactly one year later, on 18 July 1988, it was also accepted by Iran, even though the act of acceptance was two days later publicly described by the Iranian leader, Ayatollah Khomeini, presumably resting his conclusion on metaphysical assumptions, as 'more deadly than taking poison'.[1] A UN team immediately proceeded to negotiate a formal end to the fighting. A fragile peace had at last been brought to the Persian Gulf. Why had Iran and Iraq been at war, and what contribution did the United Nations make to the ceasefire to which they both eventually agreed?

THE GULF WAR, 1980–1987

The Gulf War started in a serious way when the forces of the Iraqi leader, Saddam Hussein, crossed the border with Iran on 22 September 1980 in the expectation of a brief campaign lasting one month at the most. What prompted Baghdad to take this gamble, which led to a war in which at least a million people were to die?

Pro-Western Shi'a Persian on the one hand and pro-Soviet Sunni Arab[2] on the other, Iran and Iraq had long been uneasy neighbours. Prior to 1975 the Shah, with help from the CIA and the Israelis, had been supporting the Kurdish revolt in northern Iraq, while the Ba'ath socialists in Baghdad were supporting anti-Pahlavi forces, in a supreme irony even giving refuge to the Ayatollah Khomeini. As well as being tempted into mutual domestic interference by political and religious differences, Iran and Iraq also had serious border disputes. One concerned sovereignty over the Shatt al-Arab waterway, which runs for about 60 miles between the two countries into the Persian Gulf and provides Iraq (in strong contrast to maritime Iran) with its only outlet to the oil-shipping lanes. The other involved Zain al-Qaws and Saif Saad, strategic heights overlooking the Iraqi plains which were occupied by Iran.[3]

In 1975 a comprehensive settlement of Iraqi–Iranian differences was reached with the assistance of Algerian mediation. Under the Algiers agreement the occupied heights were to be returned to Iraq, both parties agreed to desist from interference in the other's internal affairs, and the border along the Shatt al-Arab was fixed along the midstream, or thalweg, line. However, despite their relief at the Shah's agreement to stop supporting the Kurds, the Iraqis remained dissatisfied with the settlement over the Shatt,[4] believing that the accord as a whole reflected Iran's position as the American-backed regional great power at the time. Nevertheless, during these years serious military conflict was always highly unlikely. Iraq was under no threat from Iran, which was a status quo power, while Iraq itself was deterred from attacking its larger neighbour by the unfavourable distribution of power. However, as Chubin points out, 'these conditions changed drastically with the Revolution in Iran'.[5]

Following the overthrow of the Shah and the creation of the Islamic Republic of Iran, Iraq's neighbour, which had been 'secular, conservative and pragmatic', became instead the focus of a fanatical Muslim revival which rejected the lawfulness of the concept of state in favour of the community of believers. Tehran's new-found missionary zeal was directed especially at the oppressed Shi'a Muslims of the Middle East, who happened to constitute at least half of the population of Iraq. Not surprisingly, Baghdad, now finding itself attacked by the Ayatollah and his followers for secular ways and oppression of the Shi'a, became acutely alarmed, much as the European capitalist states became alarmed at the possible impact on their working classes of the exporting of the ideas of the Bolshevik revolution from Russia after 1917. Neither were Iraqi feelings towards Tehran alleviated by the fact that the Iranians had failed to return the heights of Zain al-Qaws and Saif Saad, as promised in the Algiers accord.[6]

At the same time that Iraq felt threatened by the new regime in Tehran it saw what it thought was a golden opportunity to cripple it. There were three main reasons for this. First of all, Iran had lost its powerful friends in the West (especially the Americans), while Iraq's regional and international standing had recently improved considerably. In other words, Iran, in strong contrast to Iraq, was virtually isolated. (Libya supported Khomeini and he had an 'alliance' with Syria. However, the Syrian relationship was based only on mutual animosity towards Iraq and if an Iranian victory were to have seemed imminent, Damascus – which had problems with its own fundamentalists – would probably have switched sides.)[7] Secondly, though support for the revolution was strong within Iran, there remained opposition to it. This meant much domestic turmoil as well as the existence of a fifth column which could be cultivated with advantage. Thirdly, and most importantly of all, the military balance had swung markedly in Iraq's favour. This was substantially a result of the Khomeini regime's inability to believe that such an inferior state as Iraq could possibly attack Iran, together with its religious and political contempt for modern weapons and conventional armed forces. These were regarded as weak instruments compared to the voice of the Imam and were in any case intimately associated with Western materialism and the predilections of the hated Shah. The result of this is graphically summed up by Chubin. 'In the first year of the revolutionary government . . . outstanding orders for arms were cancelled, existing projects were cut back and the government sought to find a way of selling back to the United States its F-14 aircraft. Military preparedness soon became impossible', he continues, 'as the officer corps was purged of some 10,000 senior officers by September 1980, and conscription was reduced. The military, regularly vilified and manifestly distrusted as royalist and pro-Western, were being largely replaced by a more loyal Revolutionary Guard (*Pasdaran*) . . . Weapons systems were allowed to deteriorate without adequate servicing or spare parts, and voices in favour of refurbishment were treated as counter-revolutionary and suspect.'[8] In addition, garrisons on the Iraqi border were under strength, most of Iran's tanks were deployed elsewhere, and the doctrine of 'people's war' was adopted, which was hardly appropriate as a response to a limited conventional thrust. In short, as Chubin concludes, 'Iran combined all the characteristics necessary to provoke a neighbour': it destabilised the region but simultaneously dropped its guard.[9]

Having seen the mirage of opportunity and decided to attack, Saddam Hussein, who had unilaterally abrogated the Algiers agreement on 17 August, saw his better-equipped and more mobile forces make rapid advances. However, within weeks his *blitzkrieg* had faltered, and over the next two years the numerically superior Iranians, hurling wave after wave of fanatical troops into the fighting, recaptured most of their lost territory and began to take the war into Iraq. Hussein had misunderstood the nature of Iranian nationalism and underestimated the force of the Iranian revolution, which welcomed war as its first great test.[10] After that the struggle sank into a First World War stalemate of mud and mustard gas, the Iraqis on the whole managing to hold their ground by virtue of superior armour and air power, increasing resort to chemical weapons, and the difficulties imposed on Iranian attempts to exploit breakthroughs by logistical weaknesses.[11]

In early 1984, searching for flanks in what was now unmistakably a war of attrition, Iraq launched the first 'War of the Cities' together with air attacks on ships trading with Iran. This provoked Iranian retaliation in the form of seaborne attacks against oil tankers belonging to Iraq's allies, Kuwait and Saudi Arabia. In the following year the 'Tanker War' was accompanied by a major escalation in missile attacks on population centres – the second 'War of the Cities'. In 1986 the war began to turn slightly in favour of the Iranians. The Faw Peninsula, at the head of the Gulf, was seized from Iraq in February, and a year later Hussein also lost ground at Basra, Iraq's only port. But Iran's failure to take Basra in February 1987, in yet another 'final offensive', was probably the turning point of the war.[12] By this time it was becoming obvious to everyone, including the pragmatists in Tehran, that neither side could win this war in any meaningful sense, while the human and economic costs mounted. Nevertheless, the war aims of the two sides appeared to preclude any possibility of a ceasefire, let alone a political settlement. This was especially true of the Iranians, who insisted not only on the removal of Hussein but also on an admission of Iraqi responsibility for the start of the war.

At this juncture, in the first part of 1987, the superpowers became directly involved in the conflict for the first time. The Russians allowed the Kuwaitis to charter three of their oil tankers, the Americans agreed in principle to re-flag Kuwaiti vessels under the

Stars and Stripes, and an American destroyer was mistakenly hit by a missile from an Iraqi aircraft. What were the attitudes of the superpowers to this conflict?

THE COMMON INTEREST OF THE SUPERPOWERS IN A GULF PEACE

The deep hostility of the United States to the new Islamic republic in Iran, encouraged especially by the imprisonment of American diplomats in their embassy in Tehran (which began in November 1979 and lasted for 444 days), did not, of course, lead to an automatic siding with Iraq. Saddam Hussein was, after all, a long-standing Soviet client, even though Afghanistan and disappointments with the quantity and quality of Moscow's material assistance in his war effort had put the relationship under strain.[13] Moreover, in line with traditional policy, Washington was anxious to avoid any actions which might make Iran more receptive to the embrace of the Soviet Union, while its attitude was also complicated by the need to take increasing account of Iranian influence over the fundamentalist groups in Lebanon which held hostage American citizens, as the subsequent arms-for-hostages scandal revealed. However, concerned with a vital Western interest in the region's oil, the United States was also determined to prevent Iranian aggression and fundamentalist revolution against the small, conservative states in the Gulf Cooperation Council. This required preventing an Iranian victory over Iraq. American policy in the first years of the Gulf War was thus to maintain a nominal neutrality (which would preserve the option of a future rapprochement with Iran) while in practice tilting towards Iraq.[14] A peace which preserved the status quo in the region together with a more moderate direction to policy in Tehran was the general goal of its policy.

The United States itself did not supply arms to Iraq, though it did nothing to discourage other states – such as France, Egypt and Brazil – from doing so. It was also America's friends and allies – especially France, the Gulf States and Saudi Arabia – that provided the most vital financial, commercial and transit assistance to Iraq. For its own part, the United States worked to improve relations with Iraq by extending trade credits, sharing intelligence, and (in 1985) normalising diplomatic relations.[15] By contrast, until Colonel Oliver North entered the scene,[16] Washington sought to prevent arms reaching

Iran, kept Iranian assets in the United States frozen, and made no serious effort to re-establish formal diplomatic relations. However, when the United States went to the lengths of reflagging Kuwaiti vessels in 1987 and leading a build-up of Western naval power in the Gulf in order to protect neutral shipping from Iranian attacks, the 'tilt' to Iraq had become much more pronounced. For this meant an open-ended military commitment to prevent an Iranian blockade of the Gulf states which was bound to lead to direct conflict with Tehran.[17]

The attitude of the Soviet Union towards the Gulf conflict was in certain essentials identical to that of the United States. Like Washington, Moscow had no desire to see the momentum of the Islamic revolution accelerate by means of a military triumph over Iraq. As well as destroying the remnants of Soviet influence in this important Middle East state and calling into question the value of Soviet support for 'radical' Arab states in general, this would probably have disturbing implications for the stability of Moscow's southern Muslim republics. As a result, while its closeness to Iraq (which had banned its own Communist Party and come out more strongly for non-alignment) was not what it had been, as already mentioned, the Soviet Union did not hesitate to supply Saddam Hussein with major quantities of arms when he was forced onto the defensive in 1982.[18]

As well as sharing the American objective of preventing an Iranian victory in the Gulf War, the Soviet Union was equally anxious to avoid a total impasse in relations with the dangerous ayatollahs, since an Iraqi victory over them seemed impossible. (Soviet diplomats also had been kidnapped by Iranian-backed groups in the Lebanon.) However, while not without obstacles to overcome (Iranian contempt for Soviet atheism, hostility towards the invasion of Afghanistan, and above all anger at Soviet support for domestic opposition groups and Iraq[19] Soviet overtures to Tehran were more readily accepted than American ones, especially during 1985–6 when Iran's economic situation began to deteriorate badly and the United States began to tilt more towards Iraq.[20]) Formal diplomatic ties continued more or less as usual, and in 1985 a thaw in economic relations between the two countries began to develop, though until 1987 it seemed that in practice this would amount to little.[21] Moscow's Warsaw Pact allies also became major arms suppliers to Khomeini.[22] During 1987 an agreement was also reached under the terms of which Iranian oil would be exported via a pipeline going north through the Soviet

Union. As Barry Rubin points out, the Soviet position in the Gulf War was analogous to the American one in the Arab–Israeli conflict: it could deal with both sides while the other superpower could deal only with one.[23] This difference contributed to a measure of mutual distrust between the superpowers over their respective intentions in the Gulf but it did not destroy the basis for common action laid by their common interests in the region.

THE PASSING OF RESOLUTION 598, 20 JULY 1987

Within days of the Iraqi invasion of Iran in September 1980 the Security Council had met to discuss the conflict and at the second of its meetings, on 28 September, adopted resolution 479. This called for an immediate end to the fighting and urged acceptance of mediation. However, since it contained reference neither to 'Iraqi aggression' nor to the need for withdrawal to internationally recognised frontiers, the Iranians would have nothing to do with it.[24] By 24 October, after a further four meetings, the Security Council formally abandoned the Gulf War until nearly two years later.[25]

It is not difficult to understand why the United Nations was unable either to prevent the outbreak of the fighting or to do anything to help in stopping it for many years afterwards. First, the superpowers may soon have developed a common interest in preventing an Iranian victory but this was offset by the bad relations which prevailed between them in the first five years of the war. Secondly, while at least one side felt able to win at an acceptable cost, it was highly unlikely that both would accept an offer of mediation from the UN – or, for that matter, from any of the variety of other parties anxious to help.[26] And thirdly, Iran believed (rightly) that the Security Council was prejudiced against it. This was mainly a result of resolution 479 and the Council's subsequent tardiness in condemning Iraq's use of chemical weapons.[27] (In his memoirs, Kurt Waldheim advances the fantastic argument that to have called for a withdrawal to internationally recognised boundaries would have meant taking 'a position on the substance of the dispute' at too early a stage and thus have undermined the neutrality of the Security Council.)[28] It did not help either that Kurt Waldheim had paid a courtesy visit to the Shah less than a year before the revolution, and had appeared as the agent of the United States in the subsequent American embassy hostages crisis.[29] Not until Iranian forces had begun to threaten an invasion of

Iraq, during the course of 1982, did the Security Council once more begin to call for an end to hostilities. This only deepened Iran's sense of grievance against it, and while all of its resolutions were welcomed by Iraq, they were either rejected or ignored in Tehran.[30]

As King and others have pointed out, Iran's profound suspicions of the Security Council made it inevitable that any UN role in a settlement or amelioration of the Gulf conflict would probably have to be played by the Secretariat. This is what happened. Kurt Waldheim himself, handicapped by his association with the Shah and obviously scarred by his unhappy personal initiative to resolve the hostages crisis ('Nightmare in Teheran' is the title of the first chapter of his memoirs), was not the person to head this effort. Instead he chose the ex-Socialist Prime Minister of Sweden, Olof Palme, and deputed to assist him Diego Cordovez, the somewhat vain but ambitious and able senior Secretariat official who had coordinated the UN mission on the hostages crisis and was subsequently to play a leading role in the Afghanistan negotiations. But Palme's efforts, made even more difficult by the absence of Security Council authorisation,[31] proved useless and after a final visit to the region in February 1982 (his fifth) he abandoned the mission.[32]

Pérez de Cuéllar was more acceptable than Waldheim in Tehran but his own efforts to mediate in the conflict were equally hampered by Iranian peace terms (especially the insistence on the removal of Saddam Hussein) and hostility to the UN. It is true that he had some small successes, such as arranging a partial truce that stopped attacks on civilian and maritime targets for nearly nine months during 1984.[33] However, after this moratorium collapsed, the 'eight-point plan' which he presented to the parties (a comprehensive peace proposal of the kind first suggested by Olof Palme) ran into trouble with both Iran and Iraq, and prior to 1987 there seemed little prospect that it would make much headway.[34]

In January 1987 Pérez de Cuéllar took a new initiative. This was designed to exploit the deepening stalemate in the war and the mounting evidence that the superpowers were prepared to join forces in promoting a settlement; it was perhaps also encouraged by the recent decisions of Iran's supporters, Syria and Libya, to endorse the call for a ceasefire.[35] First the Secretary-General called for an urgent discussion of the Gulf War by the Security Council, meeting at foreign minister level. Secondly, he publicly repeated the longstanding suggestion that Iran's grievance against the UN should be addressed by the appointment of an *ad hoc* committee of the Council to investigate the question: who started the war?[36]

The Secretary-General had timed his intervention well, for the superpowers, with their own direct involvement in the conflict increasing, were now inclined to take moves to end the Gulf War more seriously. In the event, it seems to have been the Reagan administration, which was also anxious to reduce congressional opposition to the transfer of Kuwaiti tankers to the protection of the American flag, which took up the call and assumed the lead in seeking Security Council action – this time backed by sanctions. (Though Sir Geoffrey Howe subsequently claimed in the House of Commons that it was Britain which had 'set the process in hand', in autumn 1986.)[37] France, whose attempts to normalise relations with Tehran had recently foundered on revelations of Iranian-sponsored terrorism in Paris, and which happened to hold the Presidency of the Security Council in July, was also pressing for tough action to end the war.[38] Equally inclined to a firm attitude towards Iran was Britain, which seems to have played the role of 'coordinator' of the five permanent members.[39]

The Anglo-American-led effort to produce a ceasefire entailed lengthy informal consultations among Security Council members in New York, together with a visit to Moscow by General Vernon Walters (United States ambassador to the UN) at the end of June and beginning of July, further American–Soviet talks in Geneva in early July, and high-level Soviet–Iranian and Soviet–Iraqi contacts.[40] (Russia, it will be remembered, was the only superpower talking to both sides.) By mid-June a draft resolution had been agreed by the permanent members of the Security Council and efforts were then concentrated on selling it to the rest of the membership.[41] On 20 July these efforts were crowned with success when the Security Council passed resolution 598, with a description of which this chapter began. This was widely viewed as more comprehensive and above all more evenhanded than its 1980 predecessor.

In the lengthy process of negotiating this resolution, the sanctions which the United States had hoped it would contain – especially an arms embargo – had been removed. This was probably conceded on the insistence of the Soviet Union and China, both of which, as major arms suppliers to the parties, would have seen their own influence over the conflict diminish. Nevertheless, it was a far stronger ceasefire call than any of the previous seven. It was passed under Chapter VII of the Charter and was thus mandatory. Accordingly, its reference to the possibility that the Security Council would 'consider further steps to ensure compliance' if necessary (widely understood to mean an arms embargo) was a real threat to the Iranians. And the resolution was passed unanimously, with seven foreign ministers in attendance.[42] George Shultz, US Secretary of State, said in the debate that the United States would support decisive application of enforcement measures should either or both parties reject the Council call.[43] Several days later the United States escorted the first convoy of American-flagged Kuwaiti tankers through the strait of Hormuz. What was the reaction of the parties to the conflict?

Iraq said that it would accept the ceasefire at once, provided Iran did the same. But Iran did not immediately accept it, arguing that procedurally as well as substantively it contained 'fundamental. defects and incongruities'; on the other hand, it said that it would consider the resolution carefully[44] and sought to build up its credentials for being constructive by inviting the Secretary-General to Tehran for talks. Prevarication was a shrewd move, no doubt designed to prevent the Security Council from adopting an arms embargo while simultaneously permitting a continuation of the war on land. Meanwhile, Iraq would be under pressure to end the tanker war, which was the greater threat to Iran. This is precisely what happened,[45] though the lull in the tanker war following the passing of resolution 598 did not last beyond the end of August.

SECURING AGREEMENT TO THE CEASEFIRE, JULY 1987–AUGUST 1988

Once resolution 598 had been passed on 20 July, the diplomatic lead in securing its acceptance was assumed, at the request of the Security Council, by the Secretary-General. However, despite the pressure on him, Pérez de Cuéllar was only too well aware of the obstacles presented by Iran's attitude and was not anxious to squander his political and other resources by a premature visit to the Gulf.[46] He was probably not encouraged either by the hostile tone towards the Security Council of Iran's formal response to resolution 598, which was finally delivered to him on 12 August by Dr Said Rajaie-Khorassani, head of Iran's eight-strong permanent mission to the UN.[47] However, following what must have been moderately encouraging talks with the Iranian Deputy Foreign Minister, Mr Mohammad Jawad Larijani, in New York on 25 August, and consultations with the Security Council shortly afterwards, the Secretary-General was instructed to visit the Gulf as soon as possible.[48] (Despite Iranian hopes to the contrary, his mandate was restricted to persuading the Iranians to accept the ceasefire resolution and did not permit re-negotiating its terms.)[49] His departure was preceded by press reports that the Security Council, exasperated by Iranian procrastination and the renewal of the attacks on shipping which occurred at the end of August, had privately agreed to approve an arms embargo should his mission fail.[50] This was probably a condition for permitting the visit insisted on by Washington, which on 1 September had threatened to push for an arms embargo against Iran unless it accepted the ceasefire within four days.[51]

Pérez de Cuéllar visited Tehran from 11 to 13 September and Baghdad for a stay of similar length immediately afterwards. In both capitals he presented an 'outline plan' for implementation of the ceasefire call. In Tehran he had 'very detailed and very cordial talks with the Iranian leadership', according to a UN official, but predictably ran into Iran's refusal to contemplate acceptance of a formal ceasefire unless the Security Council first labelled Iraq as the aggressor.[52] Nevertheless, returning to UN headquarters in New York on 16 September, Pérez de Cuéllar suggested in his report to a private session of the Security Council on the evening of the same day[53] (almost immediately leaked), that Iran might be weakening. It would not accept a *public* ceasefire until the international tribunal had pronounced on responsibility for starting the war but it would accept an 'undeclared' one. This was taken to mean that Iran had dropped its previous demand that the toppling of Saddam Hussein was the *sine qua non* of a ceasefire. Iraq maintained its acceptance of the resolution as it stood.[54]

Unfortunately, the Secretary-General's diplomacy was thrown off course only four days later when the Iranians were caught red-handed by the Americans in an action which they had always previously denied: sowing mines in the Gulf. The Americans seized the responsible vessel and on the following day, 22 September, were attacked ferociously in the General Assembly by the Iranian President, Ali Khamenei. Among other things, Khamenei reiterated the old Iranian demand for the punishment of Saddam Hussein for starting the war and, while praising the zeal and objectivity of Pérez de Cuéllar, described the Security Council as 'a paper factory for issuing worthless and ineffective orders'.[55] Immediately the Americans, backed by the British (who at last closed Iran's arms procurement agency in London), began to draft a Security Council resolution imposing an arms embargo on Iran.[56]

The next important development at the UN was a private meeting on 25 September between the Secretary-General and the foreign ministers of the five permanent members of the Security Council, who, like President Khamenei of Iran, happened to be in New York for the opening of the new session of the General Assembly. (This meeting took place just eight days after the appearance of Mikhail Gorbachev's startling article on the need to strengthen the role of the United Nations.) The meeting appears not to have given Pérez de Cuéllar precise guidance on his next move, and – in the face of opposition from the Soviet Union, supported by China, Japan and West Germany – also failed to support the Anglo-American demand for a swift move to sanctions. Nevertheless, the meeting formally endorsed the so-called 'dual track' approach: mediation by the Secretary-General stiffened by the threat contained in Security Council *informal discussion* of a draft arms embargo against Iran.[57] In theory this clearly meant that the Russians and the Chinese would no longer stand in the way of such an embargo if the Iranians continued to prove obdurate.

However, despite vigorous support by the British and the Americans, and energetic mediation by Pérez de Cuéllar in October, December and the following April, the 'dual track' approach failed. The first reason for this was the obvious reluctance of the Soviet Union, despite Eduard Shevardnadze's promise of 25 September, to go along with an arms embargo even though Iran continued to prevaricate over acceptance of resolution 598. Such a move would destroy Soviet influence in Tehran, which was now of even greater importance because of the need to obtain an undertaking of Iranian non-interference in Afghanistan in the event of a Soviet withdrawal – increasingly Moscow's top priority. (Iran contained almost a million Afghan refugees and was a key supporter of the *mujahidin*.) It is true that Moscow subsequently implied that it would support an arms embargo if this were to be accompanied by the replacement of the Western navies in the Gulf by a UN naval force[58] but it seems likely that this was designed largely for propaganda purposes. After all, despite some support for the idea in the Western press, it was always a foregone conclusion that the Western powers would never countenance the increased Soviet influence in the region that such a change would entail – nor the chaos which their prejudices led them to think a switch to 'UN control' would bring in its train.[59]

The second reason for the failure of the dual-track approach was a shift in the balance of international sympathy from Iraq towards Iran in the first part of 1988. In late February Iraq, clearly frustrated at the lack of diplomatic progress, resumed the War of the Cities; it was also using chemical weapons again. 'As a result,' observed the British House of Commons Foreign Affairs Committee, 'the mood of members of the Security Council changed, and unanimous support for the Security Council to proceed with enforcement against Iran dissolved'.[60]

Fortunately, this did not matter, for the Iranians were becoming more inclined to accept resolution 598 as a result of a more threatening development than an arms embargo: an adverse turn in the tide of battle. Iran had the worst of the renewed War of the Cities, which in March brought the conflict for the first time to Tehran itself; and it was forced into serious retreat in the land war for the first time since the opening phase of the war. In the middle of April, in a well-planned and efficiently executed operation, elite Iraqi forces recaptured the Faw Peninsular. Shortly afterwards came Iraqi successes opposite Basra, in the Majnoon marshes, and at Mehran in the northern sector. By early July 1988 both sides were more or less back where they started in September 1980, and as a result Iran had less reason to object to resolution 598: it now happened to be roughly where the resolution wanted it to be, on the 'internationally recognised frontier'.

At this juncture war-weariness was also becoming more obvious in Iran and the morale of its poorly coordinated armed forces began to sink – a factor of great concern to Tehran since it was in this quarter that it had always had the edge over the better-equipped Iraqis. Neither were Iranian spirits fortified by rumours that Ayatollah Khomeini was terminally ill and did not have long to live. It was against this background that the more pragmatic Hojatoleslam Ali Akbar Hashemi Rafsanjani, the powerful Speaker of the Majlis, Iran's parliament, achieved ascendancy over the direction of the war in early June and prepared to make concessions to bring it to an end. Given the nature of politics in Iran and the shrewdness of Rafsanjani, it would also be astonishing if he had not calculated that it would be better to terminate the war while the seriously ill Ayatollah was still able to give his blessing to the decision.

In April Pérez de Cuéllar appears to have come close to persuading the Iranians to accept the UN's ceasefire call (hardliners in Tehran were reported to have baulked at the last minute),[61] but in the event he had to wait for another three months before winning his prize. At this juncture an incident occurred which helped Rafsanjani to move decisively towards a settlement. On 3 July an Iranian civil airliner was accidentally shot down over the Gulf by a United States warship; all 290 people on board lost their lives. This simultaneously generated sympathy for Iran and allowed it to claim vivid confirmation that its war was unwinnable because it was really fighting the superpowers; this action, said Rafsanjani, represented 'America's declaration that it might commit huge crimes if Iran continued the war'.[62] The corollary of this was also valuable to Tehran: since recent defeats had really been inflicted by the United States rather than Iraq, seeking peace with Baghdad was honourable as well as prudent. Finally under cover of seeking UN condemnation of the American 'crime', Iran was able to return to the Security Council, which it had been boycotting since October 1981.

At Iran's request, a special meeting of the Security Council was held between 12 and 15 July. Attended by George Bush, the US Vice-President and Ali Akbar Velayati, the Iranian Foreign Minister, the ostensible purpose of this was to discuss the shooting down of the Iranian airliner. What emerged, however, to the considerable surprise of the outside world, was Iran's unconditional acceptance of resolution 598.

But this was hardly the end of the story. Iraq naturally suspected that the Iranians only wanted a breathing space in which to recuperate before launching a fresh offensive of their own. They were also obviously reluctant to surrender the military initiative that they had recently obtained. As a result, it was now the turn of Baghdad to drag its heels over the ceasefire, using the argument that Iran should first of all accept the humiliation of agreeing to direct talks at foreign minister level (not mentioned in resolution 598) on a comprehensive peace settlement. This, it said, would provide earnest of Iran's seriousness of intent. Nevertheless, on 8 August, having conducted difficult talks with the Iraqi Foreign Minister, Tariq Aziz, in New York, Pérez de Cuéllar was able to announce that a ceasefire would come into effect on 20 August.[63] Though there has been little progress towards a peace settlement since then, despite many rounds of direct negotiations *'under UN auspices'*,[64] that ceasefire still holds at the time of writing.

6 The Afghanistan Accords

In the interval between the Security Council's mandatory resolution on the Gulf War in the previous July and its final reluctant acceptance by the Iranians a year later, the United Nations achieved the second major diplomatic breakthrough of this period of its renascence. This was the signing at UN headquarters in Geneva, on 14 April 1988, of the four agreements which brought to an end the eight-year war in Afghanistan. Under the first of these accords Pakistan and Afghanistan agreed not to interfere in each other's affairs. Under the second, styled a 'Declaration on International Guarantees', the superpowers promised to refrain from interfering in their affairs as well and to urge others to do likewise. Under the third, Pakistan and Afghanistan settled conditions for the voluntary return of refugees. And under the fourth, which was signed by Afghanistan and Pakistan and 'witnessed' by the superpowers, it was agreed that 'foreign' (i.e. Russian) troops would be withdrawn in stages between 15 May and 15 February 1989, and also that the good offices of the UN Secretary-General should be employed to ensure full implementation of the accords. (For the full text of the accords, see Appendix 5.) Why was Afghanistan a theatre of conflict, and what role was played by the United Nations in producing the April accords?

THE CONFLICT IN AFGHANISTAN, 1979–1988

Afghanistan, which has a long frontier with the USSR, had been to all intents and purposes a Soviet sphere of influence at least since 1953, when it became the first non-communist recipient of Russian aid. After 1973, when the monarchy was abolished, the country slowly degenerated into chaos. In April 1978 the Soviet-backed People's Democratic Party of Afghanistan (PDPA) (usually referred to in the West as 'the Afghan communist party') seized power. However, stability continued to be undermined because of acute rivalry between two factions of the PDPA – the Khalq (Masses) and Parcham (Flag) – and the anger of landowners and clergy at the hasty introduction of radical policies. The Soviet Union was unable to control this situation by indirect means, and was alarmed that in these circumstances the mullahs' revolution which had just occurred in

57

neighbouring Iran would either sweep over Afghanistan itself (with serious implications for the stability of the Muslim republics of Soviet Central Asia) or provoke an American intervention against Tehran. In the latter event, Afghanistan might be dragged into the Western orbit instead. As a result, in December 1979 Soviet forces invaded Afghanistan and installed in power the Parcham leader, Babrak Karmal.

Unfortunately for Karmal and his Soviet backers, Muslim fundamentalist sections of the population took up arms against the new government in Kabul. Over the following years the *mujahidin* slowly developed into a formidable guerrilla force and obliged Moscow to pour in more and more men and equipment to keep their puppet, whose own army was unreliable, in power. (The figure was never enormous but at the high-point of engagement Soviet uniformed forces in Afghanistan probably numbered around 120 000 men.)[1] What strengthened the *mujahidin* was the extent of their external support.

The Muslim world in general sided with the *mujahidin*, neighbouring Pakistan and Iran taking the lead because they feared that the Soviet invasion might signify a determination to move against them next. (Pakistan had long been worried by the implications for its security of Soviet activities in Afghanistan, especially the building of north–south roads and tunnels.) Two other factors pushed Pakistan into the forefront of this conflict, though they had contradictory implications for its desire to see it brought to an end. On the one hand, it was a heaven-sent opportunity for the new Pakistani president, General Zia-ul Haq, to shake off his regime's unsavoury reputation. He could now present himself as the leader of a 'front-line state' in the defence of the 'Free World', and the tangible assistance from the United States, China and Saudi Arabia which this status generated was crucial in consolidating his domestic position.[2] But on the other hand the fighting led to an influx of almost three million refugees from Afghanistan, who gave rise to considerable political as well as economic problems. One of these was the fear that a more solidified refugee movement within Pakistan would lead to an increase in cross-border support for the *mujahidin*, which might in turn provoke the Soviet Union to step up its material assistance to anti-Zia groups operating inside Pakistan. Another was the possibility that the refugees, mainly Pushtu-speaking, would resurrect the old agitation for greater autonomy from Islamabad on the part of the 7–10 million Pukhtuns in the North-West Frontier Province of

Pakistan.[3] (Large numbers of Afghan refugees were also taken by Iran.)

The United States, which repeatedly emphasised that the invasion of Afghanistan represented an extension of the Brezhnev doctrine outside the area of the Warsaw Pact for the first time, also made a major issue out of it. Aid was channelled to the *mujahidin*, who became 'freedom fighters' in the Washington lexicon as much as UNITA in Angola and the Contras in Nicaragua. American hostility was intensified by fear that the Russian thrust was a precursor to a move towards the vital Gulf,[4] and was paraded with all feathers spread in an attempt to regain the prestige which Washington had lost in the region as a result of events in Iran. The Afghanistan conflict, therefore, swiftly became a contest between the Soviet-backed Karmal regime on the one hand, and the US/Pakistani backed *mujahidin* on the other.

At first things went well for the Russians and badly for the motley *mujahidin*. But gradually the balance began to swing the other way, especially after the Americans massively increased their weapons aid to the Afghan resistance in late 1985. Especially potent in the hands of the guerrillas were the CIA-supplied Stinger missiles, which began to impair Soviet control of the air over Afghanistan during 1986. Of course, the Russians were never in danger of suffering a military defeat in Afghanistan but at this point it began to look as if the *mujahidin* would be able to tie them down indefinitely, at huge cost to the Afghan people. Already, thousands had been killed and more than a quarter of the entire population driven into foreign exile.

THE UNITED STATES SABOTAGES UN MEDIATION, 1980–1983

In the Afghanistan conflict, of course, the Security Council was in a much more difficult position than that in which it found itself in relation to the Gulf War. In the latter conflict, neither superpower was directly engaged (though America was threatening to become so) and both shared a strong interest in bringing the war to an end. In Afghanistan, by contrast, the Soviet Union was a major combatant and the conflict of interest between Moscow and Washington could not have been deeper. The Soviet Union wanted to preserve the Kabul regime while the United States wanted to see the Afghan communists removed or at least see the Russians bled white in the struggle to preserve them. (Washington's hard-line 'bleeders', as they were known, were stronger in the Pentagon and the CIA than in the State Department, though they were in the overall ascendant for the greater part of the war. Those more inclined to negotiate a settlement along the lines favoured by the UN Secretariat were normally known as the 'dealers'.)[5] As a result, while Moscow was happy – even anxious – to withdraw its forces if it could be given *guarantees* that the Americans and the Pakistanis would stop their support for the efforts of the *mujahidin* to overthrow the 'Democratic Republic of Afghanistan' (DRA), the United States and its allies in this conflict would only countenance a discontinuation of their own involvement on the understanding that the Afghans be allowed freely to choose their own government.

On top of the policy impasse between the superpowers over Afghanistan, the Soviet Union was widely attacked for having started the war, which did not encourage Moscow to lend a sympathetic ear to those calling for its end. In light of these considerations, and bearing in mind that the Soviet veto, like that of the United States during the Vietnam War, stood squarely in the path of any substantive proposal to which it took objection, it is not surprising that in this instance the Security Council proved unable to agree on a ceasefire resolution or on guidelines for a peace agreement. Nevertheless, the Russian decision to pull out of Afghanistan, according to the American scholar Selig Harrison, was not only a result of pressure from the *mujahidin* but of '7 years of farseeing and determined United Nations diplomacy'.[6] Since this is undoubtedly true, how did it come about?

An attempt by the non-aligned nations in early January to persuade the Security Council to call for the withdrawal of 'all foreign troops' from Afghanistan was predictably vetoed by the Soviet Union, and the debate was switched to an emergency special session of the General Assembly. Here the first of many calls for withdrawal was overwhelmingly supported a week later, but it was not until November 1980, when the Assembly specifically directed the Secretary-General to appoint a 'special representative' to promote a political solution, that any chance of diplomatic progress became possible.

The auguries for the first special representative, who was in fact Pérez de Cuéllar, at that time Under-Secretary-General for Special Political Affairs, were not good. This was because the corollary of Russian hostility to the General Assembly resolution was hostility to the appointment of a special representative charged with promoting a settlement under its terms. However, Kurt Waldheim overcame Soviet resistance on this point by re-styling the appointment that of 'Personal Representative'. 'This deliberate ambiguity', he records in his memoirs, 'would allow one side to assume that I was proceeding as directed by the Assembly while the other side could assume ["pretend" would have been more accurate] that I was not'.[7]

During the first half of 1981, following a visit to the region by Pérez de Cuéllar in April and another to Moscow in the company of Waldheim in May, the Russians and the Afghans indicated that they were prepared to accept the 'good offices' of the Secretary-General in negotiations between Kabul and Islamabad, provided the *mujahidin* did not participate.[8] Negotiations through the UN had the advantage for the Russians of reinforcing the legitimacy of the DRA, since it was the accredited government of Afghanistan in the General Assembly.[9] Nevertheless, during a further trip to the region in August, Pérez de Cuéllar was unable to move the deadlock.

In the following January Pérez de Cuéllar was elected Secretary-General and passed his Afghanistan portfolio to Under-Secretary-General for Special Political Affairs, Diego Cordovez. An Ecuadorean who had worked at the UN since the early 1960s and rarely returned to his home country, Cordovez acquired a reputation for being ambitious and extremely sensitive to press criticism.[10] Nevertheless, his competence had been highly rated by Waldheim,[11] and Pérez de Cuéllar presumably concurred in this judgement. Harrison describes Cordovez as 'an international civil servant of unusual political acumen' and believes that he brought more drive and willingness to goad to the UN mediation than his more 'cautious' superior.[12]

In his memoirs, written at a time when no progress towards a settlement in either the Gulf or Afghanistan seemed imminent and all of the laborious UN diplomacy seemed to many to be meaningless, Kurt Waldheim observed that 'In every international dispute, a window of opportunity eventually opens and the moment occurs when accommodation is possible. If,' he continued, 'through quiet, intensive diplomacy, the issues have been clarified, the potential points of compromise explored, the underlying objectives and priorities of the contending parties investigated, the possibility of agreement is enhanced.'[13] This is also the doctrine to which Cordovez clearly subscribed, and it is not a bad one; it served him well.

In August 1981 Pérez de Cuéllar had already made some progress on procedural points,[14] and in the first visit to the region by Diego Cordovez, in April 1982, the format and agenda of the talks was agreed. Negotiations, to be held at UN headquarters in Geneva, would proceed 'indirectly', with Cordovez mediating between Pakistan and Afghanistan (assisted by Russian 'experts'). This arrangement, which was unavoidable in view of the refusal of Pakistan to recognise the Soviet-backed regime in Kabul, required that the parties should never be in the Palais des Nations at the same time: 'One delegation had to leave before the other could be invited to meet with mediator Cordovez'.[15] (The UN and the Pakistanis had also wanted the Iranians to participate formally in the Geneva talks. However, this had been refused by Moscow because Tehran wanted to put the objective of securing an Islamic republic in Afghanistan on the agenda,[16] while the Iranians had refused to participate in any case as long as representatives of the resistance were excluded.[17] It became established practice for Iran to be kept informed through the Iranian permanent representative to the UN office in Geneva.) As for the issues for negotiation defined in April 1982, these were identical to those on which the Geneva accords focused five years later. Cordovez also secured agreement at this time that in view of the interrelatedness of the issues the target should be a 'comprehensive settlement'.[18]

Following the agreed format, the foreign ministers of Afghanistan and Pakistan held discussions with Cordovez for the first time in June 1982. According to the UN Secretariat, these achieved understandings on 'the possible structure and contents of the settlement';[19] the deal which was implicit in the agenda was beginning to emerge.[20] This was a Soviet troop withdrawal in return for an end to external assistance to the *mujahidin*. Consistent with the status of the DRA as a UN member government, it was *not* part of Cordovez's thinking that the DRA's demise should be written into the settlement (the fate of Karmal himself was another matter). Nor was it a part of his concept that the DRA should cease to continue receiving economic and military aid from Moscow after the Soviet withdrawal.[21] At that stage, at any rate, it was inconceivable that this would ever be countenanced by Moscow. Geopolitical considerations aside, the Russians claimed that, unlike aid to the *mujahidin*, their own aid to the DRA had legal status under bilateral agreements going all the way back to the Afghan–Soviet Friendship Treaty of 1921.

The death later in 1982 of Leonid Brezhnev, the Soviet leader who had ordered the invasion of Afghanistan, and indications of greater flexibility on the part of his successor, Yuri Andropov, led to a wave of speculation that the prospects for a diplomatic settlement had improved significantly. Further reasons for the change in outlook were the deepening military stalemate and mounting concern in Pakistan that failure to achieve a settlement would provoke Moscow into stepping up its material support to anti-Zia forces. At Brezhnev's funeral in November there were encouraging conversations between Zia and Andropov.[22] Shortly afterwards, Andropov also impressed Brian Urquhart with his greater flexibility.[23] Nevertheless, there remained important obstacles to progress. The chief among these, of course, was the difficulty of reconciling Moscow's need to obtain international guarantees that the DRA would not be overthrown once the last Soviet troops had been withdrawn, with Washington's desire to witness precisely such a debacle. To this extent, the Afghanistan negotiations were an echo of Kissinger's need to secure assurances during his negotiations with the North Vietnamese in the early 1970s that the Saigon government would not be overturned on America's departure from Vietnam. Nevertheless, as in these negotiations, the possibility of a coalition government began to feature in the Afghanistan discussions as a way out. Indeed, Moscow was by now indicating that it would consider this 'later in the settlement process'.[24]

Against a background which was at any rate relatively promising, in early 1983 Cordovez had talks in Islamabad, Kabul and Tehran, during which he produced the first unified outline of a draft settlement along the lines which had been emerging in the previous year.[25] Two further rounds of proximity talks in Geneva, in April and June, focused on this draft. In April, Moscow indicated that Karmal could be sacrificed and that a specific timetable for the projected withdrawal of its troops would be suggested at the next round. In return, Pakistan implicitly agreed to recognise the DRA and cut off aid to the *mujahidin* when the Soviet troop withdrawal began.[26] By this time, according to Cordovez, 95 per cent of the four-point draft accord had been agreed,[27] and the air was full of talk of a possible breakthrough.

But the June round did not seal this emerging deal, and the deadlock persisted. This was almost certainly a result of sabotage by the United States, abetted by Saudi Arabia and China. Washington not only objected to the omission of provisions for ensuring genuine Afghan self-determination from the UN plan but – despite public claims to the contrary – secretly feared that the DRA might survive in modified form after a Soviet withdrawal.[28] Moreover, even within the

State Department most officials believed that Moscow was exploiting the UN-sponsored negotiations 'merely to buy time and reduce external pressure while consolidating control over Afghanistan',[29] overlooking the distinct possibility that Moscow could have seen these advantages as merely *extra* attractions to diplomacy. In any event, according to Harrison, 'the divided Reagan administration did little to help Cordovez, often insinuating that he was being used for Soviet propaganda purposes. In early 1983 . . . the administration sent negative signals ranging from skepticism to bitter hostility. Eager to keep American military aid to Pakistan flowing, Islamabad reneged at the last minute on earlier understandings with Cordovez. Andropov's professed readiness to withdraw was never tested . . .'[30] Shortly after the June failure, Pérez de Cuéllar revised downwards Cordovez's estimate of the degree of agreement from 95 per cent to 90 per cent![31]

'A CAR WITHOUT AN ENGINE': BUILDING THE ACCORDS, 1984–1985

Following the disappointment of his hopes during the first half of 1983, Diego Cordovez appears to have made it one of his priorities to persuade the Pakistanis to move nearer to direct talks with Kabul. This was important because Moscow and Kabul were also beginning to cool on the UN negotiations, insisting in particular that they could place no faith in Pakistani promises of non-interference unless Islamabad placed this on record in a bilateral treaty with the DRA.[32] In this, at least, the UN mediator had some small success. During a visit to the region in April 1984 he secured agreement that the format of the negotiations should be changed from 'indirect' to 'proximity' talks. This meant that henceforth, while Cordovez would still be needed as a go-between, the Afghan and Pakistani delegations would now at least be present at UN headquarters in Geneva *at the same time*, albeit seated in separate rooms; this made the negotiations less laborious as well as signifying a small concession on the part of Islamabad.[33] (The use of the terms 'indirect' and 'proximity' in this context was confusing because 'proximity talks', of course, are also indirect.)

At the end of August 1984 the first of many rounds of 'proximity talks' was held in Geneva, and here Cordovez had another small but significant success. He persuaded the Pakistanis (who did not inform the Americans of this in advance) to permit the agreement on non-interference to be embodied in a bilateral treaty between Islamabad and Kabul, as the Russians sought, instead of in a 'declaration of understanding' issued in the name of the UN.[34] But this round was more notable for its disagreements. The Pakistanis privately accepted at this time the suggestion being canvassed by Cordovez that outside aid to the *mujahidin* should stop at the same time that the Soviet withdrawal began (the 'Day One' formula), but Moscow and Kabul continued to insist that it should precede the withdrawal.[35] They also adamantly refused to consider a Pakistani proposal that Moscow enter its signature to a Kabul-Islamabad agreement on the troop withdrawal, insisting that since the troops had been invited in by the DRA their withdrawal was only the business of Moscow and Kabul.[36] For its part the Soviet Union suggested that the embryonic settlement's international guarantees should take the form of a joint US–Soviet statement in which the superpowers would not only pledge their own future restraint from intervention in Afghanistan and Pakistan but their cooperation in resisting any intervention by third parties. This was a considerable advance on the UN draft's suggestion under this heading (which provided merely for separate statements in which the superpowers pledged self-restraint), and appears to have made no headway.[37]

The next step forward did not come until a year later, after Mikhail Gorbachev had become Soviet leader and Moscow adopted a slightly more accommodating attitude. During 1985 Washington also began to send out more conciliatory signals, emphasising its interest in a settlement and its recognition that the Soviet Union had a legitimate security interest in the nature of the regime in Kabul.[38] This took place against the background of the 'fresh start' which President Reagan now claimed to be seeking in relations with Moscow. (It was in October 1985 that he informed the General Assembly of his hope that this would lead to superpower cooperation in bringing 'regional conflicts' to an end.)

The proximity talks in June 1985 were described by Cordovez as 'very intense, serious and fruitful'.[39] The Soviet representative indicated that, by means of a procedural compromise, Moscow would in effect co-sign the instrument governing the withdrawal (the 'fourth instrument') rather than insist that Kabul alone should sign.[40] He also agreed to accept Cordovez's formula that the aid cut-off should coincide with 'Day One' of the Soviet troop withdrawal. By the end of this round, the detailed content of the first three agreements (on non-interference, guarantees and the voluntary return of refugees) had been substantially agreed. There was a further round of proximity talks in late August, and Afghanistan was also discussed at the first Reagan–Gorbachev summit in November, following which the President told Congress that his administration had decided to 'intensify' its meetings with the Soviet Union on regional conflicts.[41] On 13 December the State Department gave its public blessing to the emerging deal on Afghanistan by revealing that the administration had written a letter to Cordovez agreeing to act as a guarantor. Deputy Secretary of State John Whitehead, who made this announcement, added only one condition: that the terms of the Soviet withdrawal should be right.[42]

But once more Cordovez, not to mention the long-suffering Afghan people, had to endure a false spring. Powerful elements within the Reagan administration, including the CIA, appear to have remained convinced that the Russians had absolutely no intention of pulling their troops out of Afghanistan, and that the UN-mediated negotiations were still little more than a Soviet propaganda exercise. Hence, rather than signifying the imminent success of the negotiations, the American offer to act as a 'guarantor' appears to have been seen by the administration as nothing more than 'a harmless psychological-warfare gambit' which would keep the Russians on the defensive in the negotiations.[43] As for the Moscow-Kabul axis, this was now firmly indicating its refusal to agree to a withdrawal timetable until Pakistan signified its recognition of the DRA by agreeing to direct talks (though it hinted that it was considering withdrawal over three to four years).[44] This had already caused serious difficulties in the August talks,[45] and it continued to block progress on the vital 'fourth instrument' at another round of proximity talks in mid-December.[46] *The Economist* of London summed up the state of the negotiations in late December 1985 rather neatly when it said that 'the agreement so far is a little like a car without an engine. A lot of work has gone into putting together the body, and all the pieces are now in place except the one that will make it go – an agreement on the withdrawal of Russian troops'.[47]

THE LAST LAP, 1986–1988

Afghanistan was not the Soviet Union's Vietnam. By early 1986 Moscow had only about 120 000 troops in the country compared to the 550 000 that the United States had in Vietnam by 1968; these troops amounted to only about 2.5 per cent of overall Soviet force strength and represented a mere 1–2 per cent of defence expenditure. Soviet casualties were much lighter than those of America, and their opponents were hardly in the same military class as the North Vietnamese and the Vietcong. The Soviet Union, moreover, did not face anything like the domestic pressure to end the Afghan involvement which confronted the Johnson and Nixon administrations over Vietnam. Nevertheless, as the *mujahidin* began to put to use the great increase in the American weapons flow which started during 1985, and became somewhat better organised, the military and economic costs incurred by Moscow began to mount. At the February Party Congress Gorbachev called Afghanistan 'a bleeding wound'.[48] Perhaps more importantly, the intense and broad-based international disapproval of Soviet policy over Afghanistan was beginning to be seen by Mikhail Gorbachev as a considerable obstacle to implementation of his 'new thinking' in foreign policy.[49]

It was against this background that Cordovez visited Moscow in February and made clear that troop withdrawal would have to be negotiated in the existing talks format or his mission would become 'pointless'.[50] The UN mediator may have been taking something of a personal risk here since under Gorbachev the Russians were exploring a variety of other diplomatic channels which might help them over Afghanistan, including a direct dialogue with Pakistan.[51] In any event, the Cordovez *démarche* appears to have made an impression, for on 4 May, only hours before the next round of talks were due to begin, Babrak Karmal, who had disappointed the Russians on the domestic front as well as having become the personification of the hard line on direct talks, was replaced as leader of the PDPA and the country's president. His successor was the head of the regime's ruthlessly efficient intelligence service (Khad), Dr Sayid Mohamed Najibullah. Tough, courageous, astute and charismatic, with a high tribal pedigree which had already proved a considerable political asset, Najibullah had been the key adviser to the Russians in the planning of the 1979 invasion.[52]

The next round duly took place on the usual 'proximity' basis, and on 23 May the text of the 'fourth instrument' was completed – except, as UN understatement had it, for two 'outstanding issues'. These were verification of the Soviet troop withdrawal and cut-off of aid to the *mujahidin*,[53] and the *timetable* of the Soviet troop withdrawal![54] Nevertheless, the UN mediator kept up the momentum and in

November, after failing to break the deadlock at a further round of talks in early August, was able to claim another breakthrough. The Russians told him, during a visit to Kabul, that they were prepared to accept the UN plan for a 50-strong monitoring force which would (somewhat optimistically) oversee all aspects of the settlement.[55]

Movement on the timetable had to wait until the talks were resumed in late February 1987. At this juncture Kabul improved its offer to eighteen months, while Islamabad proposed seven.[56] The gap between the sides was closing but the Soviet Union was still clearly anxious about the fate of Najibullah. A key element in its strategy, designed both to strengthen the DRA regime and encourage a settlement, thus became 'national reconciliation' inside Afghanistan.[57] (Since this meant the abandonment of communism, 'national reconciliation' also provided Moscow with an ideological pretext for withdrawal.)[58] Though the attempts made by Najibullah to broaden the base of his government which were required by this strategy never looked like succeeding, and were described as unacceptable by the United States, there were signs in the first half of 1987 that the effort was at any rate helping to break Kabul's diplomatic isolation in the third world.[59] Moreover, Najibullah had improved the performance of the government in Kabul and, most importantly, begun to make progress in rebuilding the spirit of the Afghan army.[60]

Perhaps it was with greater confidence that a PDPA-dominated government would survive after their departure that, in June 1987, the Russians took their secret decision to withdraw by 1989.[61] Nevertheless, in the following months it became increasingly obvious that Gorbachev would welcome a pre-departure coalition in Kabul even if it was dominated by non-communists – and, failing this, would be prepared to let Najibullah, albeit still provided with economic and military aid by Moscow, fend for himself after the departure of Soviet troops.[62] This led predictably to deepening tensions between Kabul and Moscow, which surfaced dramatically at the Geneva talks in September when *Pravda* undercut Najibullah's position by saying that the small concession on the withdrawal timetable which he was now offering (16 months instead of 18) was inadequate and that twelve would be acceptable.[63] Six weeks later the Russians informed Washington that they had abandoned their insistence that the formation of a coalition government should precede their withdrawal.[64] Following this, on 29 November Najibullah publicly accepted the one-year withdrawal timetable, and it is reported that this was confirmed during discussions between Gorbachev and Reagan at the December summit in Washington.[65]

Events were now moving rapidly. The White House reacted to Gorbachev's offer by demanding a starting date for the withdrawal. (Under enormous Congressional pressure, it was now openly accusing the 'dealers' in the State Department of proposing to betray the *mujahidin*.) Cordovez, anxious to strengthen the hand of supporters of the nearly completed accords, begged Moscow and Kabul to respond with a firm, 'front-loaded' timetable offer. The results exceeded even the expectations of the 'super-optimistic'[66] UN mediator. On 8 February 1988 Mikhail Gorbachev announced that the Soviet withdrawal would begin on 15 May, if the accords were signed by 15 March. Moreover, not only would the 'greater portion' of Soviet forces be pulled out in the 'first phase' but the whole withdrawal would be completed in ten months rather than twelve.[67] Undoubtedly aware of the controversy in Washington over the 'asymmetry' of the 'Day One' cut-off in aid to the *mujahidin* regardless of the fact that Moscow would be allowed to continue giving aid to Kabul, and more especially of the controversy over whether the United States was already committed to this which went back to the events of December 1985,[68] Gorbachev was clearly seeking to use the moral high ground to bounce the Americans into accepting 'asymmetry'.

This set the scene for what turned out to be the last round of proximity talks in Geneva, accompanied by top-level bilateral talks between Moscow and Washington. Not surprisingly, this round was also the longest, for the Reagan administration refused to accept 'asymmetry', and the Russians in turn accused the Americans of backsliding on earlier understandings. Moreover, each superpower had to deal with important differences with its client. In the end, after negotiations were almost abandoned and Cordovez was required to make great exertions to keep them going, the Russians accepted a highly disadvantageous fudging of the symmetry issue – Washington would be allowed to continue aiding the Afghan resistance, though it would employ 'restraint' in the exercise of this 'right', provided Moscow was restrained in its aid to Kabul (see Appendix 5).[69] This enabled all four instruments to be signed in Geneva on 14 April, on which day the Pakistanis finally agreed that the talks should become direct. All instruments would enter into force on the target date set earlier by Mr Gorbachev, 15 May, and the withdrawal of troops would be completed within nine months rather than ten. One half of the troops would be withdrawn by 15 August, that is to say, within the first three months.

Cordovez had finally won his settlement. The Geneva accords did not settle the conflict between Najibullah and the *mujahidin*, who roundly denounced them.[70] Moreover, there is force in the argument advanced by Rosanne Klass in a prescient article in summer 1988 that 'the Geneva negotiations and the resulting accords have provided a solution to the wrong problem: an arrangement for the long-term Soviet consolidation of control in Afghanistan without the overt use of its uniformed military forces, and in a manner satisfactory to world opinion'.[71] But by getting Soviet forces out of Afghanistan the Geneva accords also substantially reduced the harm that the issue had inflicted on superpower relations. As US Secretary of State George Shultz said at Geneva, faithful implementation of the withdrawal commitment by the Soviet Union would 'do much to improve the atmosphere for our bilateral relations and for the resolution of other regional conflicts'.[72] Moreover, the Soviet withdrawal was also likely to improve relations between the Soviet Union and China and the Soviet Union and the Islamic world, not the least of whose members was Iran. At this particular juncture, therefore, the signing of the UN-brokered Geneva accords, which allowed the Soviet Union to pull out of Afghanistan without major damage to its prestige, was a development of the greatest significance.

7 The Angola/Namibia Settlement

On 22 December 1988 two agreements were signed in New York which brought to an end over two decades of fighting in the south-western corner of Africa (see Appendix 7). The first, which was signed by Cuba, Angola and South Africa, set 1 April 1989 for the beginning of the implementation of UN Security Council Resolution 435, which had been passed over a decade earlier, on 29 September 1978 (see Appendix 6). This contained a plan for achieving the independence of Namibia, the ex-German colony of South-West Africa which was seized by the South Africans during the First World War. Under this plan, a 7500-strong UN force was to be inserted into the territory. The object of this would be to guarantee suitable conditions for the holding of 'free and fair elections' for a constitution-making assembly seven months after implementation of the resolution commenced. Formal independence would follow shortly afterwards.

The second agreement provided for the total withdrawal of Cuban troops from Angola in stages by July 1991, and, following the precedent established in the Geneva Accords on Afghanistan signed earlier in the year, was cast in face-saving form. As in Geneva a veil was drawn over the influence of outside powers on the decision of the Russians to withdraw their troops from Afghanistan by presenting the agreement in question as one concluded merely between Moscow and Kabul, so the agreement on Cuba's withdrawal was signed by Cuba and Angola alone in order to support the fiction that South African actions had had no bearing upon it. Implicit in both agreements, it is also important to note, was a non-aggression pact similar to those which South Africa had signed with neighbouring countries (including Angola) earlier in the 1980s. In return for South Africa dropping Jonas Savimbi's UNITA (the Angolan 'contras'),[1] the African National Congress (ANC) would be refused permission to operate not only from Angola but also from Namibia, where SWAPO (the South-West Africa People's Organisation) was expected to come to power following independence.

The December agreements, while by no means perfect, were more carefully designed than some came to fear after the flare-up of fighting in northern Namibia in early April 1989, and made possible the independence of Namibia in early 1990. However, with only a handful of notable exceptions,[2] contemporary press accounts gave credit for achieving these agreements overwhelmingly to the development of favourable circumstances, though references to the 'dogged patience' of the mediator, US Assistant Secretary of State for African Affairs, Dr Chester A. Crocker, sometimes entered as an afterthought. As for the contribution of the United Nations, this was either minimised or ignored altogether.[3] Of course, circumstances and diplomatic qualities – and energy and political imagination for that matter – were vital, but it is also likely that these agreements would not have seen the light of day if certain characteristic ploys of diplomacy had not been employed with great skill by the states concerned. It is also probable that they would not have been so easily constructed in the absence of the United Nations. What was the background to the conflict? What was the role in the settlement of the United States, the Soviet Union and Britain? And what was the contribution of the UN?

THE BACKGROUND

The fighting in south-western Africa had initially been confined to South Africa and SWAPO, the 'liberation movement' which was contesting Pretoria's control of Namibia. Later, however, the fighting engulfed Western-and South African-backed UNITA and its rival, the Marxist (MPLA) regime which came to power in Angola in 1975 with the military support of Cuba and the material and diplomatic support of the Soviet Union. SWAPO and UNITA, both operating in southern Angola but competing for different prizes, were for many years 'blood brothers'. They fell out after the MPLA success, when UNITA was forced to rely more and more on SWAPO's enemy, South Africa, and SWAPO had little choice but to throw in its lot with UNITA's enemy, its host government, the OAU-recognised MPLA regime in Luanda.[4] By the second half of the 1970s, then, the regional line-up had cemented itself into South Africa and UNITA versus Angola (MPLA), Cuba and SWAPO.

Various attempts, both inside and outside the framework of the United Nations, had been made to bring an end to this conflict prior to 1987–8, but it was not until then that circumstances for a settlement became especially propitious. In the first place, the military stalemate which had existed for years was made more than usually obvious by the outcome of the battle for Cuito Cuanavale, the Angolan government's southernmost fortified air base, 150 kilometres north-west of UNITA's front line at Mavinga in Cuando Cubango province. In the latter half of 1987 the Angolans, after two years of relative quiescence, launched their biggest-ever set-piece assault on UNITA positions in the south-east of Angola, reportedly designed to extend a 'Maginot line' of government defences as far east as the Zambian border, thereby cutting off UNITA guerrillas fighting on the new northern front from their headquarters at Jamba.[5] However, the Angolans were stopped by UNITA with the assistance of massive help from the South African Defence Force (SADF), and the government forces were beaten back to Cuito Cuanavale. Here it was the turn of the Cubans to put in major reinforcements, the SADF/UNITA advance was halted and what had threatened to become a swift rout turned into a protracted siege: 'Angola's Stalingrad'.

Having been held at Cuito Cuanavale, in the biggest conventional battle southern Africa had ever seen, in mid-1988 the SADF suffered two further embarrassments: first, the threat that its forces inside Angola would be cut off when the crack Cuban 50th Mechanised Brigade suddenly deployed almost on the Namibian border; and secondly, the successful demonstration of Cuban air power in the attack on the SADF-guarded Calueque dam on the Angolan side of the Namibian border. (South Africa's own air force was increasingly feeling the strain of the arms embargo.) White casualties were also reaching politically serious levels but had not assumed the proportions that might have impeded the search for a settlement by requiring Pretoria to make unrealistic demands in order to justify the sacrifice. By this time, then, the military situation was not only disposing the South Africans to think more seriously of diplomatic solutions but also to abandon their earlier dreams of making their forces in Angola their main bargaining chip[6] and instead fall back on the offer of independence for Namibia. At the same time, the failure of their biggest ever push against Savimbi demonstrated to the Angolans that the South Africans would not let him go under and that there was no prospect of a military victory in the Angolan civil war.

By early 1988 the fighting in southern Angola was also exacting an increasingly burdensome economic cost, particularly on Angola and South Africa but also on the Cubans and their Soviet patrons. The economy of Angola was being badly damaged by declining oil and diamond revenues, while each Cuban in the country, according to American sources, was costing Luanda $10 000 a year. With the major Cuban reinforcements which had recently been poured in (bringing the total figure for Cuban forces to about 50 000, twice its size at the beginning of 1985) the bill had been rising dramatically. Virtually all of Angola's oil revenues were going on the war, and its economy was literally disintegrating. As for South Africa, the economy of which had been in recession for a number of years, the war was believed to be costing it more than $1m a day, together with a subvention to the interim government in Windhoek which Pretoria claimed was about $400m a year.

If Angola and South Africa were being forced to seek a diplomatic solution (for mainly military and economic reasons), the Cuban leader, Fidel Castro, who had of late been re-emphasising that his forces would remain in southern Africa until apartheid itself was toppled, was now inclined to be flexible as well. This was because he was able to present the battle for Cuito Cuanavale, in which Cuban forces had played such a decisive role, as the turning point not only in the Angolan war but in the whole history of Africa.[7] (If the history of Africa is seen principally in terms of the struggle between black and white, Castro may well prove to have been right.) With the 30th anniversary of his revolution also approaching, Castro was in triumphant mood and was clearly not apprehensive that withdrawal of his troops from Angola, provided it was staged over a long enough period, would risk any loss of face. Significantly, a photograph of 'the victorious internationalist generals' seated in the Cuban delegation at the signing of the December accords accompanies the publication of their full text in the international edition of the Cuban Communist newspaper, *Granma*.[8]

Other parties whose attitudes were likely to have a bearing on the prospects for a settlement were also in pacific mood. Savimbi, for one, was disinclined to use spoiling tactics, despite being kept out of the negotiations on the insistence of the MPLA, which hated and feared him. This was because the US government, following the repeal in 1985 of the Clark Amendment,[9] had used renewed arms supplies and routes through friendly Zaire in order to obtain a much firmer hold over his movement relative to the influence traditionally exerted over it by the South Africans. As for SWAPO, militarily weak, heavily dependent on Cuban and MPLA support, standing to win perhaps the biggest prize of all, and initially encouraged by

Luanda to believe that it would play a formal role in any negotiations with the South Africans,[10] it was obviously in no mood to stand in the way of any such talks. Zambia and Zaire, too, were particularly anxious to see an end to the war so that the Benguela Railway could be re-opened (Savimbi had offered this in March 1987 but been overruled by Pretoria).[11]

Above all, the superpowers themselves had entered a new era of cooperation during 1987 and 1988, as we have seen in the two preceding chapters. By the time that the Angola/Namibia negotiations got under way seriously, in the middle of 1988, this cooperation had already borne fruit in Afghanistan and the Gulf. Superpower determination to cooperate in the settlement of expensive and dangerous 'regional conflicts' was to have an equally decisive impact on the settlement in south-western Africa, and in important respects the 'Afghanistan model' provided a guide. It is even probable that the Soviet Union, where voices less hostile to the retention of ethnic criteria in the South African constitution were beginning to be heard, was now intimating to Pretoria that it would repay a South African withdrawal from Namibia with pressure on the ANC itself to seek a negotiated solution to the whole question of apartheid.[12] Britain, too, the traditional paramount external power in southern Africa, was as ever anxious for peace in the region.

It is obvious, therefore, that circumstances in mid-1988 favoured a settlement over Angola and Namibia. However, it is also apparent that significant barriers to a settlement remained. In particular, the MPLA was afraid that a deal which involved the departure of the Cubans but did not also include the cessation of both South African and American support to UNITA would result in the swift overthrow of its government. However, while the South Africans, who had normally been very coy about their support for UNITA anyway, might have had no difficulty in dropping Savimbi, especially if a quid pro quo in regard to the dropping of support for the ANC was offered by Luanda, this hardly applied to Washington. The Reagan administration, after all, had publicly committed itself to the support of UNITA while the Soviet Union continued to backstop the MPLA, and Moscow and Luanda were parties to a longstanding Treaty of Friendship and Cooperation. The MPLA regime was also apprehensive that, in the event of the collapse of a comprehensive settlement, simple geography meant that the SADF would be able to return to the fray far more quickly than the Cubans.

For their part, the South Africans were extremely reluctant to surrender the huge bases in northern Namibia which put them in such an excellent position to intimidate not only Angola but (bearing in mind Caprivi) the whole of south-central Africa. They had also found the war an excellent source of sophisticated Soviet weaponry, and good testing for their own troops and home-made equipment. Above all, the Botha government was apprehensive about the response of white voters, already deserting to more right-wing parties over its domestic policies, to any settlement likely to result in the hated colours of SWAPO being hoisted over Windhoek. This argued for the swift departure of the Cubans to allow Botha to claim a victory over the Communists (precisely what Castro could not allow), and provisions which would effectively eliminate the influence of SWA-PO fighters in any elections held in Namibia under UNSCR 435 (precisely what the SWAPO leader, Sam Nujoma, could not allow). Clearly, there remained a major task for diplomacy.

THE AMERICAN ROLE

Though the Angola/Namibia accords had their origins in contacts between the parties earlier in the 1980s, they were chiefly the product of ten rounds of publicly announced negotiations which began in May 1988, secret talks held in Cape Verde in late July, and 'informal talks' in New York in early October. Of this total of twelve rounds, at least ten were chaired by Chester Crocker in the role of official American mediator between the Angolans and the Cubans on the one hand, and the South Africans on the other. In establishing and maintaining contact between the two sides, it is also important to note that the Americans were unobtrusively assisted by their close allies, the British, who (unlike the United States) had an embassy in Luanda, were held in high regard by the South Africans for holding out against sanctions, and had a claim to be taken seriously by SWAPO since it was assumed that an independent Namibia would apply for membership of the Commonwealth.[13]

Mediation by one power, the United States, had the advantage of greater decisiveness over the fractious Western contact group which had led the negotiations in the late 1970s and early 1980s.[14] Moreover, Chester Crocker benefited from a greater degree of impartiality than he has sometimes been credited with, doubts on this score having arisen because the United States was a partisan of UNITA, the Angolan regime's bitter domestic opponents.[15] In fact, despite attempts by the MPLA regime in the early rounds to put US support for UNITA on the agenda, probably encouraged by US concessions made under this head in the Mindelo Minutes agreed in January 1984,[16] Crocker substantially succeeded in keeping it off. He achieved this not least by emphasising its linkage to Soviet support for the MPLA and encouraging parallel talks on the civil war brokered by regional members of the Organisation of African Unity (OAU). Indeed, the State Department was increasingly emphatic that, while it favoured reconciliation talks between the MPLA and UNITA, the Angolan civil war was a *separate issue*; what was on the table was only a Cuban withdrawal from Angola in return for a South African withdrawal from Namibia. (For this reason, as well as because Savimbi's presence could not be countenanced by the MPLA, UNITA did not participate in a single round of the negotiations.) In short, while it is true that Washington's identification with UNITA to some extent affected its standing in the Angola/Namibia talks, the exclusion of the civil war from them rendered this less important: the United States *was* partial in this war but the civil war, on the model of the Afghanistan settlement, was not the issue.

With regard to the conflict between the Angolans and the Cubans on the one hand, and the South Africans on the other, Washington was more impartial. The MPLA regime in Luanda was not recognised by the US government, it is true, but this had not prevented the State Department from having close contacts with it for a long time, as it had with Communist China between 1971 and recognition in 1979. In addition, American companies played an important role in Angola, not least in its vital oil industry, and Angola's ties with the capitalist world were strengthening all the time. Perhaps most strikingly of all, Washington firmly resisted the temptation to take a public stand against the major build-up of Cuban troops in southern Angola which coincided with the first half of the negotiations, a decision which even led some commentators to speculate that this Cuban move may have been encouraged by Washington in order to put more pressure on the South Africans.[17] On the other side, the US government was applying limited sanctions to South Africa under the Comprehensive Anti-Apartheid Act, 1986, and had so lost the confidence of Pretoria that, as will be seen, it tried to cut the United States out of the talks. Crocker himself was regarded by the Republican right as too pragmatic and an apologist for terrorism in Africa, and had held up his confirmation in the early months of the Reagan administration.[18] Moreover, he had initially opposed the repeal of the Clark Amendment for fear that this would drive the MPLA away from the talks.[19]

But was American mediation – or mediation by anybody for that matter – really necessary? The parties to the conflict were, after all, clearly capable of grasping the principle mooted by the Americans, in the early months of the Reagan administration, that Namibia's independence should be 'linked' to the withdrawal of Cuban troops from Angola. The Angolans, as well as the South Africans, had also signified their acceptance of the *principle* itself in late 1984.[20] Moreover, in contrast to the situation in Afghanistan, where the Pakistan government refused to recognise the Najibullah regime and thus made direct, face-to-face talks impossible, in the first half of 1988 the Angolans and the South Africans both showed themselves willing to cut the Americans out of the negotiations altogether and hold direct talks.[21] This actually happened in Brazzaville on 13 May, when South Africa's Foreign Minister, Pik Botha, and its Defence Minister, Magnus Malan, met an Angolan delegation led by Justice Minister, Fernando van Dunem.[22] It is also possible that it happened in the highly secret Cape Verde talks.[23]

It is true that the South Africans showed themselves much more willing than the Angolans to do without US mediation, and also that their display of willingness may have been merely a temporary tactic designed, inter alia, to put pressure on the United States for a more friendly attitude towards their various demands. The fact remains, however, that the Angola/Namibia talks were clearly not mediated by the Americans because Luanda and Pretoria were incapable of establishing contact without them. Instead, the United States more or less *imposed* its mediation on them because the Reagan administration was anxious to take the credit for removing the Cubans from Angola and generally to underline America's indispensability in the settlement of regional conflicts. This could be expected to pay diplomatic dividends not only in the Soviet Union and the Middle East but also in Africa itself, which would understand from which direction the wind was blowing. (Speaking in London in April 1989, Crocker claimed that, since the Angola/Namibia settlement, 'the American flag flies high in Africa'.)[24] Successful mediation in Angola would also have great advantages for the Republicans in domestic politics. It would improve the chances of George Bush in the presidential election in November,[25] and it would help to get Congress (threatening a stronger sanctions package in the Dellums Bill) off its back by presenting a victory for the battered policy of 'constructive engagement' with South Africa.

Having said all this, it remains unlikely that, in the absence of American mediation, such a comprehensive settlement would have been achieved so quickly, if at all. The main reason for this is connected to the fact that without a mediating role in 1988 the Americans would not only have lost their chance to take the credit for a settlement but, given their eight-year pursuit of one, suffered a serious blow to their prestige. This dismal prospect would have substantially reduced their anxiety for a settlement and commensurately reduced the pressure for one which they exerted on both Luanda (via the advantages in terms of economic aid of US recognition[26]) and Pretoria (via the threat of the White House to drop its opposition to the Dellums Bill[27]). In the absence of direct US involvement in the talks and the sustained top level consultation on them with Moscow of which this was the practical corollary, it is also possible that the Russians would have put less pressure for withdrawal on the Cubans.[28]

The importance of Crocker's mediation was perhaps seen most vividly in the third round of talks, at Cairo in June, where he was supported in the wings by Vladillen Vasev, head of the Southern African Department of the Soviet Foreign Ministry.[29] These talks took place against a background of rising military tension in southern Angola (following reports of a build-up of Cuban troops near the Namibia border), and witnessed furious exchanges which spilled over into the issue of apartheid itself.[30] Had it not been for the presence of Crocker, it seems highly likely that the negotiations might have foundered in Cairo. These events also demonstrated that, while the MPLA had shown itself reluctantly willing to be seen talking alone to the South Africans, there was a serious question as to whether the Cubans, who in any case had least to gain from the settlement taking shape, would have been prepared to do the same. Following the fourth round of talks, in New York, which took place only three weeks after those in Cairo, American mediation was explicitly and publicly acknowledged by the Cubans, Angolans and South Africans to be one of the fourteen principles which were 'indispensable' to a peaceful settlement of their conflict. Perhaps significantly, the breakthrough made during round eight, at Geneva in mid-November, on the key issue of the timetable of Cuban withdrawal, was made on the basis of a compromise proposal put forward by Chester Crocker.[31]

If mediation was necessary to settle the conflict in south-western

Africa, and American mediation backed by Britain and the Soviet Union proved its potency, this was also assisted by American employment of a diplomatic procedure popularised (or at any rate publicised) by Henry Kissinger in an earlier Republican administration: *linkage*, or negotiating on a broad front.[32] This approach to the solution of the problems of south-western Africa had not been supported by the United Nations and had indeed been roundly condemned by the friends of SWAPO and the MPLA ever since it had first been recommended by the United States at the beginning of the Reagan administration. Why, it was argued, should the Angolans be obliged to eject the Cubans, invited in to afford them protection in the face of a South African invasion, in order to secure the independence of Namibia – which under international law South Africa was in any case obliged to grant? This was simply not right, and was merely a ruse designed to put off indefinitely the day when SWAPO would come into its inheritance.[33] How, nevertheless, did linkage help the Angola/Namibia negotiations (even though it may have contributed indirectly to SWAPO's subsequent disastrous decision to cross the border into northern Namibia on 1 April 1989[34])?

By winning the point that, despite profound juridical differences, the issues of South African withdrawal from Namibia and Cuban withdrawal from Angola were *in fact* related, Chester Crocker undoubtedly established a vital precondition for the attainment of both. For the MPLA regime in Luanda could not, in the absence of a fundamental change in the military equation, have taken the *military* risk of accepting the departure of its Cuban guards while the SADF retained its formidable presence in northern Namibia and southern Angola (where it was able to give close support to UNITA); nor could the Botha government have taken the *electoral* risk of pulling out of Namibia without being able to flourish in front of potential defectors to the Conservative Party the quid pro quo of Cuban (and ANC) departure from Angola. Here, then, was a real rather than a cynically contrived linkage, though the widespread and prolonged resistance to the idea during the 1980s shows that even real linkages have to be actively nurtured.

THE ROLE OF THE UN

The United Nations had wrestled with the problem of Namibia virtually since the foundation of the organisation, most recently with the so-called 'Western contact group' making the running. This consisted of the three Western permanent members of the Security Council – America, France and Britain – and the two non-permanent members of the Council, West Germany and Canada, who had seats during 1977, when the group was established. However, the contact group was doomed from the moment the election of Ronald Reagan in November 1980 took the pressure for a settlement on the existing terms off the South Africans,[35] and over the next two years it slowly disintegrated.[36] Since the negotiations which brought success in December 1988 were dominated by an American team not even nominally flying UN colours, it is not surprising, therefore, that the United States would take all the credit and the contribution of the UN would be overlooked. This was all the more likely since a major objective of the Republican administration in Washington, which was facing an election in 1988, was precisely to get the credit for bringing peace to southern Africa.[37] Nevertheless, the UN made a real contribution to ultimate success.

In the first place, as the Americans have since half-acknowledged, Chester Crocker's mediation effort had been relieved of a major burden by the Western contact group and by the United Nations. As Chas. Freeman, a leading member of his team, has admitted: 'There was no need to negotiate the terms of the South African withdrawal or Namibian independence; these had already been spelled out in 1978 in U.N. Security Council Resolution 435'.[38] In other words, some fairly precise *guidelines* for a partial settlement had already been created, and Freeman might have added that these included constitutional guidelines as well.[39] In view of the inevitable complexity of the 'linkage' strategy, he might also have put more emphasis on the importance of having agreed these points already. Crocker himself had the decency to say afterwards that linkage 'would build on what had already been achieved – which was substantial.'[40]

Of course, it might be replied to the above argument, as the State Department's Freeman does, that the achievement of the Western contact group, led by the USUN team headed first by Andrew Young and then by Donald McHenry, was not so much an achievement of the UN as 'a major achievement of American alliance diplomacy'.[41] And it is certainly true that this *was* in substance an essentially NATO operation. This is why it had standing with the South Africans and why, conversely, it was regarded by the Soviet Union as simply another device of the imperialists, who it believed to be in league with the South Africans, to frustrate the popular struggle.[42] (It was only in order to avoid giving offence to the front-line states in Africa that they abstained on resolution 435 rather than veto it.) *But the UN was the focus of the contact group's efforts and the group itself had a clearly visible UN pigmentation.*

The top echelon of the contact group consisted of senior representatives of the five Western states in New York. (The second tier – or 'parallel' section – of the contact group was made up of the ambassadors of the five in Pretoria/Cape Town.)[43] It also operated explicitly as the executant – albeit self-appointed[44] – of a whole series of UN resolutions on Namibia, most recently Security Council Resolution 385 of 30 January 1976. Furthermore, the group liaised closely with the UN Secretariat, and as early as June 1977 its efforts were openly endorsed by the Organisation of African Unity.[45] Consistent with the UN focus, early in the Carter administration responsibility for Namibia was shifted from the African Affairs Bureau of the State Department to the International Organizations Bureau.[46] The UN Secretariat itself, it should also be noted, partnered the contact group in mediating between South Africa, the internal Namibian parties and SWAPO once resolution 435 had been secured. Had it not been for the election of Ronald Reagan, Secretariat efforts, spearheaded by Brian Urquhart, could have been especially fruitful in late 1980 and early 1981.[47] Furthermore, in August 1983 Pérez de Cuéllar was sent by the Security Council to southern Africa in order to try, in the event unsuccessfully, to break the deadlock.[48] And in September 1988 the Secretary-General, who had been remarkably successful in distancing himself from the political organs of the UN in the Namibia case,[49] which was of great importance in view of the longstanding South African charge of 'UN bias', once more visited the region. This time he reinforced the American-led effort by publicly reaffirming, in South Africa, his determination to give no special privileges to SWAPO in the forthcoming Namibian elections.[50] But why was the United Nations the unavoidable *focus* of the contact group's efforts, and why did the group find it advisable *to operate under the name of the UN*?

One reason, extraneous to the immediate problem, why the UN was made the focus of the contact group's efforts should not be overlooked. Jimmy Carter, the new American President, liked the organisation. Addressing American officials serving at the UN on 4 October 1977, he claimed that 'more and more, there has been a realisation that without the U.N. there could be no resolution of any regional disputes and problems . . . I, myself, have a deep commitment to the United Nations and want to see its role expanded in the future.' Continuing, he remarked that 'It hasn't always been a fact that the U.N. could take the major responsibility in a potential trouble spot like Namibia and retain that role . . .', and he added that in Zimbabwe 'we and the British are very eager to see the United Nations come in and play a larger and larger role'.[51] There were, however, particular reasons why the contact group decided to concentrate on the UN, and the main one was made clear by David Scott, who was the first British member of the South African end of the contact group.

The United States and the EEC agreed, records Scott, that 'it was essential to tackle the problem at the main point of international pressure – i.e. at the United Nations'.[52] This was obviously true. New York was the unchallenged focus of agitation about Namibia. As the last surviving major colony, the territory was of great symbolic importance to the African group in the General Assembly.[53] The Assembly, through its Council for Namibia, had even assumed legal responsibility over it. If a settlement was not endorsed in New York, it would not stick. On the practical level, it also made sense to focus the negotiations on New York because of the presence at UN headquarters of a mission from Angola, with which the United States had no formal relations. Not surprisingly, this is the point at which channels of communication were built to the MPLA government, which was in turn of such importance in influencing SWAPO.[54] Finally, a UN focus was advisable because the Security Council had determined that the organisation itself would play an important administrative and policing role in the transition of the colony to independence. This meant that the Secretariat would be deeply involved in negotiations on the 'modalities' of this arrangement. But it was one thing for the contact group to focus its activities on the UN; it was quite another for it to assume a UN garb. What were the advantages of this?

It was important that the contact group display a tinge of UN blue in order to encourage SWAPO's stubborn and deeply suspicious leader, Sam Nujoma, to take it seriously. Apart from bolstering the group's claims to impartiality, mediation within a UN framework was important to its credentials with SWAPO because it was the endorsement of the UN rather than military exploits against the SA Defence Force which was the chief source of Nujoma's authority. Any attempt to negotiate outside the UN, in other words, would have implied non-recognition of SWAPO's special status and thus vitiated any attempt by the West to bring him to terms with South Africa. In this context it is important to remember that during the heyday of the contact group, in contrast to the later period, SWAPO was *under no pressure from the Soviet Union to cooperate* with Western diplomacy (though it was from the front-line states), and 'the armed struggle' was generally in much greater vogue.

In addition to playing an important role by providing the framework within which a substantial part of the settlement had already been negotiated ten years before peace was finally brought to south-western Africa, the UN also made a significant contribution in the later stages of the negotiations. In the first place, the status of the Soviet Union and the United States as 'permanent members of the Security Council', rather than as great powers naked of international rectitude, clearly made it politically easier for them (relative to each other, relative to their clients, and relative to the world at large) to pose as plausible 'guarantors' of any settlement, and there seems little doubt that this had lubricated Chester Crocker's diplomacy during 1988. (The Angolans, who were being asked to surrender their Cuban guards, seemed especially anxious on the matter of guarantees, as might have been expected.)

The first clear indication that superpower guarantees, suitably adorned in UN accoutrements, would have a role to play in an Angola/Namibia settlement was provided in the fourteen principles of July. These included 'Recognition of the role of the Permanent Members of the Security Council of the United Nations as guarantors for the implementation of agreements that may be established,' together with 'the onsite verification' of any Cuban troop withdrawal by the Security Council as well.[55] Subsequently, an annex to the Brazzaville Protocol of 13 December spelled out the agreed procedure for creating a 'Joint Commission', in which the superpowers were invited to take part as 'observers', to oversee implementation of the three-party accord on Namibian independence and non-aggression.[56] (The Joint Commission was to prove its worth in holding the settlement together after SWAPO's armed entry into northern Namibia on 1 April 1989.) And in article 3 of the Angola-Cuban agreement signed on 22 December, the Security Council was invited to verify the fallback and total withdrawal of Cuban forces from Angola.[57] (The UN Angola Verification Mission, UNAVEM, had already been established by the Security Council on 20 December.)[58] In short, as in the Afghanistan negotiations, so in the Angola/Namibia talks the impression was strongly conveyed that any party seeking to undermine a settlement would incur the disfavour of both superpowers. This undoubtedly increased the confidence of each side that the other would keep to its undertakings and thus represented a vital ingredient in the resolution of the conflict. This element in the settlement would not have been impossible to contrive in the absence of the United Nations but it would probably have been more difficult.

The second contribution made by the United Nations to the final stage of the negotiations was, of course, the assistance which it gave to the Soviet Union (and indeed to the MPLA and the Cubans) to climb down without massive loss of face. Moscow had, after all, executed a complete U-turn by accepting the American principle of linking Namibia's independence to the withdrawal of Cuban forces from Angola; it had even discreetly but visibly helped to bring it to life. Had a UN patina not veiled the settlement in the end, this might have been harder for the Russians to swallow. Apart from providing for verification of the Cuban withdrawal *by the United Nations*, the December accords were themselves signed *at UN headquarters in New York in the presence of the Secretary-General*, and were soon afterwards endorsed *by the Security Council*. It might be added, too, that in the final, critical months, Pérez de Cuéllar had done much in his personal capacity to make it difficult for the South Africans to continue alleging 'UN bias' and use *this* as a pretext for further stalling.

There is, of course, no denying that in the end the Angola/Namibia accords were principally a result of the American-led efforts under Chester Crocker. But it is also clear that the UN had played its part and that the accords were the product of precisely the kind of *joint diplomatic effort* between the UN and member states with 'a special relationship' to the parties to a dispute which the Secretary-General had pleaded for in his annual report in 1982.[59]

8 The Unfinished Agenda

No one, least of all the United Nations Secretariat, would claim that the diplomatic breakthroughs made with UN assistance in the Gulf, Afghanistan and south-western Africa have settled all of the problems in those regions. In the Gulf War the achievement consisted of persuading both sides to accept a ceasefire; there is still no peace treaty. In Afghanistan the achievement amounted to getting Soviet troops out of the country; the civil war continues to rage. And while the Angola/Namibia accords paved the way for a comprehensive settlement of the Namibia conflict, they left civil war sputtering in Angola. There is, in other words, a substantial unfinished agenda even in these three regional conflicts. Nevertheless, in each of them diplomatic agreements were achieved which were widely regarded as of great importance, principally because they removed these conflicts as obstacles to improvement in relations between the Russians and the Chinese and the Russians and the Americans.

While real breakthroughs were made in these three conflicts with UN assistance, there were also others in which the UN was diplomatically engaged and in which the Secretariat began to talk hopefully of breakthroughs. This was especially true of the conflicts in Kampuchea, the Western Sahara, and Cyprus. Talked up by the Soviet Union, the possibility of a major role for the UN in an Arab – Israeli settlement – the greatest prize of all – also appeared on the horizon during this period. What contribution has the UN made to diplomatic progress in these conflicts?

KAMPUCHEA

The present conflict in Kampuchea started with the Vietnamese invasion in 1979, which was aimed at removing the genocidal, pro-Chinese regime of Pol Pot's Khmer Rouge. Confronted by one of the best armies in the world, the Khmer Rouge retreated towards the Thai frontier, herding with them thousands of civilians. Many more fled in the same direction to escape the fighting. In the end, about 300 000 refugees were settled in camps along the border, mainly on the Thai side. These were used by the Khmer Rouge as bases for military resistance to the new 'People's Republic of Kampuchea'

(PRK) which was installed by the Vietnamese in Phnom Penh under Heng Samrin. The PRK was quickly recognised by the Soviet Union but the vast majority of UN members (including the other four permanent members of the Security Council) regarded it as a Vietnamese puppet regime and insisted on allowing 'Democratic Kampuchea', i.e. the Khmer Rouge, to retain Kampuchea's seat in the world organisation. The Khmer Rouge were supported most avidly by China in order to keep their Vietnamese enemies pinned down (there were 'bleeders' in Beijing as well as Washington). But only marginally less enthusiastic for them was the non-communist Association of South-East Asian Nations (ASEAN), which represented Thailand, Malaysia, Singapore, Indonesia, Brunei and the Philippines and was apprehensive of Vietnamese expansionism. Since ASEAN was backed by the United States, which itself had no reason to love the Vietnamese, the Kampuchea conflict was another theatre of superpower rivalry, though the competition was less direct than in Afghanistan.

In due course the Khmer Rouge were joined in the struggle against the Vietnamese-backed PRK by two militarily weaker non-Communist factions. These were Prince Norodom Sihanouk's National United Front and ex-Prime Minister Son Sann's Khmer People's National Liberation Front (KPNLF). In 1982 the resistance coalition, styling itself the 'Coalition Government of Democratic Kampuchea' (CGDK) and armed by France and Singapore as well as by China, was in turn recognised by the United Nations as the legitimate government of Kampuchea.

The UN had been involved in diplomatic attempts to resolve the Kampuchean conflict at least since July 1981, when an 'International Conference on Kampuchea' was convened under General Assembly auspices 'with the aim of finding a comprehensive political settlement of the Kampuchean problem'. Chaired by the foreign minister of neutral Austria and attended in one capacity or another by 93 countries, this adopted a Declaration which called, inter alia, for negotiations on a general ceasefire, withdrawal of all foreign forces, and free elections – all under UN supervision.[1] (The Declaration was vaguely formulated in order to paper over serious differences between China and the ASEAN countries over the rights of the Khmer Rouge.)[2] Unfortunately for the prospects of a UN role in Kampuchea diplomacy, or in the policing and administration of any settlement for that matter, the Soviet Union, Vietnam, Laos, and India, together with other states aligned to the Soviet Union, refused to attend the

International Conference. The reason for this, of course, was UN policy in regard to the recognition of the Khmer Rouge as the legitimate government of Kampuchea. The view of the Phnom Penh regime was that it was the rightful government of Kampuchea and that the activities of the International Conference amounted to nothing more than 'flagrant intervention' in its internal affairs – which, of course, it was.[3] The UN had not had this problem in the roughly analogous case of Afghanistan, where the de facto government was also the one which it recognised.

As an alternative to the UN's International Conference, the Soviet Union and its three Indo-Chinese allies (the PRK, Laos and Vietnam) proposed a 'regional conference' at which they would meet the five ASEAN states together with China, France, India, the UK and the United States.[4] Not surprisingly, the most urgent tasks of the continuing organisation created by the International Conference – an '*Ad Hoc* Committee' composed of Japan, Malaysia, Nigeria, Senegal, Sri Lanka, Sudan and Thailand – were to flesh out proposals for a solution and persuade the absentees to abandon their own preferred format and instead attend the next session of the International Conference.[5]

In autumn 1981 the General Assembly adopted the Declaration made by its International Conference and also asked the Secretary-General to employ his good offices in the conflict. He in turn appointed a Special Representative, Under-Secretary General Rafeeuddin Ahmed. Facing continued opposition to a UN role, however, Pérez de Cuéllar made little progress, even though he was allowed to present his views on Kampuchea to Hanoi and Vientiane, albeit in a 'personal capacity'.[6] By 1985, if not before, it was clear that the UN's International Conference format for negotiations was a dead-end and that the Secretariat was cautiously promoting a compromise with the alternative Soviet format. In his report to the General Assembly opening in that year, Pérez de Cuéllar indicated that a consensus seemed to be emerging for 'a limited international conference' which would involve the participation of all parties directly concerned: the five permanent Security Council members and other mutually acceptable countries.[7]

The prospects for a diplomatic settlement of the Kampuchea conflict, at least in so far as this meant an end to *external* involvement in the crisis, on the Afghanistan model, improved markedly during 1987–8. This was substantially because both the Soviet Union and Vietnam were now more anxious for a normalisation in relations with

China. For the Vietnamese, whose economy was in dire straits, an end to their occupation of the country also promised an end to their general isolation (especially the aid embargoes) as well as to an exhausting and apparently unwinnable war. But like the Russians in Afghanistan, the major quid pro quo that they demanded for their troop withdrawal was a cessation in arms supplies to the resistance. For their part, the Chinese were also prepared to promote an end to the conflict but would only accept an internal settlement which gave a place to the Khmer Rouge in order to offset the weight of the Vietnamese-backed faction in Phnom Penh.

In these relatively propitious circumstances it was not, however, the United Nations which was to find it the easiest to promote negotiations. Still labouring under the hostility towards the UN of the Vietnamese and the PRK as a result of its recognition policy, Pérez de Cuéllar was obliged to witness the achievement of initial successes by initiatives undertaken both by ASEAN and the ex-colonial power, France. Starting most obviously with the Ho Chi Minh City Understanding on procedural questions negotiated between Indonesia and Vietnam in July 1987[8] and the first of several meetings in Paris between the new PRK leader, Hun Sen, and Prince Sihanouk in Paris in early December, this 'two-track' approach[9] eventually merged in July/August 1989. At this juncture a major conference on Kampuchea at foreign-minister level, co-chaired by the French and Indonesian foreign ministers, was held in Paris. Among others, the Paris Conference included all four Cambodian factions, Vietnam, the 'Big Five', and the ASEAN states – and, for some of the time, the UN Secretary-General.

With the 'Big Five' leaning on their respective clients, the aim of the Paris Conference was a peace treaty providing for international supervision of the Vietnamese withdrawal, a ceasefire between the PRK and the resistance coalition, an end to external arms supplies to the contending factions, and a 'quadripartite' transitional government charged with preparing a constitution and free elections. Unfortunately, the Conference broke up without any real breakthroughs, principally because agreement could not be reached on the role of the Khmer Rouge.[10] The war in Kampuchea continued.

What had been achieved by the two-track approach on the road to the Paris Conference, and what role had the UN played in the diplomacy? In the first place, there had been vital *procedural* progress: direct talks between the contending parties, internal and external, had been established. In the second place, as the French insisted after their

Conference, a 'framework for agreement' had been provided which would make settlement easier when circumstances were more propitious.[11] This was partially true. There had been a real breakthrough in late 1988 when the Chinese Prime Minister, Li Peng, indicated that it was inconceivable that China would continue to support the Khmer Rouge after Vietnam's withdrawal from Kampuchea. This meant Chinese acceptance, at last, of the linkage of these two issues.[12] At the second 'Jakarta Informal Meeting', held in February 1989, a target date of 30 September 1989 had been agreed for the completion of the Vietnamese troop withdrawal, and linkage had been endorsed.[13] Moreover, calculating that their withdrawal would erode the legitimacy of the Khmer-dominated resistance coalition and thus progressively starve it of support,[14] the Vietnamese had gone ahead with their withdrawal despite continued support for the Khmer Rouge by the Chinese. Inside a month of the collapse of the Paris Conference, the Vietnamese withdrawal appeared to have been completed. Part of the 'framework' of the agreement had already been acted upon! (Though failure to agree on 'international verification' of the Vietnamese withdrawal permitted the Chinese, and others, to claim that it was a sham.) Judged by the standards of the agreements on Afghanistan and Angola, which did not provide for internal settlements either but were justified principally on geopolitical grounds, the Kampuchea diplomacy was a success. It is because the Khmer Rouge are not the *mujahidin*, because, that is to say, the Khmer Rouge have a reputation for genocidal bloodletting, that there is so little satisfaction over achievements in regard to Kampuchea – and that the agenda on this conflict has to be regarded as even less complete.

As already indicated, the UN role in the achievements secured in Kampuchea up to this point had been, on the published evidence, relatively marginal. (At Paris Hun Sen refused to agree to a peacekeeping role in Kampuchea for the UN.)[15] It is true that the *Ad Hoc* Committee of the UN's International Conference visited China and Thailand in the middle of 1988[16] and Brunei and Thailand, for a second time, a year later.[17] It is also true that in mid-1988 Pérez de Cuéllar 'felt that the time had come to formulate a number of specific ideas, with a view to facilitating the elaboration of a framework for a comprehensive political settlement of the problem', and that in consequence over the next twelve months Rafeeuddin Ahmed was very active in pressing the 'good offices' of the Secretary-General on all of the parties to the dispute, as well as those with a special interest in its settlement. (During this period he paid two visits to Moscow.)[18] These various efforts probably contributed to the momentum in favour of direct talks leading to an Afghanistan-style solution. In addition, according to one report, Pérez de Cuéllar, with his prestige enhanced by the UN's successes in other regional conflicts, was a 'key performer' at the Paris Conference and was responsible for securing one of the few agreements to emerge from it: the immediate dispatch to Kampuchea of a 'purely technical' UN fact-finding mission.[19] Nevertheless, the fact remains that the French and the Indonesians bore the brunt of the attempt to mediate in this conflict, and the important meetings which were arranged were not even nominally held under 'UN auspices' – precisely what the PRK and the Vietnamese could not have allowed.

It was not long, however, before things began to change and the UN was turned to in a way that it had never been turned to before in this conflict. There were two main reasons for this. First, though there were small signs that external support to the resistance coalition might be weakening following the withdrawal of the Vietnamese troops (as Hanoi had gambled), it soon became clear that this would be unlikely to happen quickly enough to save Hun Sen from the Khmer Rouge. The resistance coalition was not ousted from Kampuchea's seat at the UN, and in late 1989 and early 1990 the Khmer Rouge began to make significant military gains in the west of the country. Secondly, the Australian government came up with a plan, which it canvassed with great energy, to side-step the obstacle on which the Paris Conference had foundered – the composition of an interim administration which would govern until free elections had been held. The idea was that United Nations officials, supported by a substantial UN military force, should assume this role; meanwhile, the Kampuchea seat at the UN would be left temporarily vacant.[20] With his military position increasingly tenuous, Hun Sen discovered a new enthusiasm for the United Nations and clutched at the plan.[21] So did Vietnam.[22]

It was against this background that the United States, which now seemed genuinely worried that the Khmer Rouge would once more overrun Phnom Penh, took the initiative in calling a meeting of the Security Council 'Big Five' in Paris to consider the Australian plan. The Russians, the British and the French were enthusiastic and the Chinese seemed prepared to listen. Meeting on 15 January, by the following day the 'Big Five' had agreed guidelines for a UN role in the transition period.[23] Of course, the Khmer Rouge were hostile and there remain enormous obstacles to be overcome in agreeing the details of the operation but, even if it fails to take off, these developments provide further evidence that there are situations in which the United Nations cannot be ignored.

WESTERN SAHARA

The conflict in this ex-Spanish colony, squeezed against Africa's North Atlantic seaboard by Morocco to the north and Mauritania to the east and south, began when Spain surrendered the territory to its two neighbours in a secret agreement of November 1975. (In 1979 Mauritania abandoned its own claims and Morocco annexed the whole territory.) Not surprisingly, the most important of the extant indigenous liberation movements, the *Frente Popular par la Liberación de Saguia el-Hamra y Rio de Oro* (Polisario), took exception to this development and in February 1976 announced the formation of the 'Saharawi Arab Democratic Republic' (SADR). Supported by Morocco's traditional regional rival, Algeria, where Saharawi refugee camps were established, Polisario has been fighting King Hassan of Morocco ever since.[24]

The Western Sahara conflict has never been especially dangerous in the context of the cold war. This is because the Soviet Union never took much interest in it,[25] while the traditional friendship of the United States with Morocco, which Washington found strategically useful and generally sound in foreign policy, was accompanied during the 1980s by a desire to develop better relations with Algeria. (This country was 'valued for its great influence in the Third World'[26] and was of help to Washington in resolving the Tehran Embassy hostages crisis.) On the other hand, the Saharan conflict has had a profoundly disruptive impact on relations between the countries of the Maghreb and, indeed, within the Organisation of African Unity (OAU) as a whole, which virtually foundered on Moroccan-led opposition to the admission to membership of the SADR in 1982.[27] The danger in the Western Sahara is that it could trigger a war between Morocco and Algeria and drag in other regional states, if not the superpowers.

As in similar conflicts, hopes for a settlement in the Western Sahara rested on the costs and futility of enduring a military stalemate. The war against Polisario certainly proved very costly for Hassan, whose strategy consisted largely of pushing steadily southwards an extraordinary electronic warfare defence line, the 'Saharan wall'.[28] By 1985 the bulk of his armed forces (120 000 men) was concentrated in the defence, support and supply of this remote 900-mile wall: as many men as the Russians committed to Afghanistan at the height of the struggle against the *mujahidin*. For Morocco, the resource costs of this strategy were enormous. So, too, were the diplomatic costs, as it found itself increasingly isolated by support for Polisario in the UN, the OAU and the Non-Aligned Movement. By 1985, the SADR had been recognised by sixty-three states, of which 31 were in Africa.[29] Moreover, the resilience of Polisario's guerrillas (approximately 20 000 men, well equipped by Algeria) suggested that Hassan's strategy was unlikely to prove effective since even if the wall were to be pushed right up to the Algerian and Mauritanian frontiers, Polisario would simply attack it from the other side. Hassan could hardly push the wall any further!

Numerous attempts to broker a diplomatic settlement in the Western Sahara, usually under the auspices of either the OAU or the Arab League, had been made before the UN Secretary-General entered the fray in the second half of the 1980s. But these had all foundered in great measure because of the intractability of the conflict. As Zartman points out, 'there seems to be little middle ground between one-sided victories: a Polisario state is an Algerian victory, and the denial of a Polisario state is a Moroccan victory'.[30] Partition of the Western Sahara between Polisario and Morocco also looks like a non-starter since the territory's population, infrastructure and wealth (its phosphate resources) are concentrated in a small zone in the north-west, the 'useful triangle'.[31] A solution apparently favoured by Zartman (he is a little coy on this), who is influenced by unexplained hostility to the appearance of another micro-state in the region and sympathy for Morocco's historic claims to the Western Sahara, is for Polisario to be forced into accepting a federal or confederal relationship between the territory and Morocco. This would be achieved at the expense of 'compensating' Algeria i.e. buying out its support for Polisario, in some unspecified way.[32] But this compensation (large American 'side payments'?) would have to be extremely hefty since Algeria would have to be asked not only to execute a U-turn on Polisario but contemplate the emergence of a greatly strengthened Morocco. A long-canvassed alternative, as we shall see, is to organise a referendum in the territory on its future. This hardly removes the power struggle, merely changes its form; nevertheless, people get killed only in the violence which accompanies negotiation of its terms and, under prevailing international norms, a referendum provides more legitimacy to the outcome of the struggle.

The position of the UN General Assembly on the Western Sahara has gone through a number of gyrations and at times it has adopted contradictory resolutions.[33] However, by the mid-1980s it was firmly behind the peace plan proposed by the OAU in June 1983. This called for direct negotiations between Polisario and Morocco aimed at achieving a ceasefire and thus the conditions necessary for a 'peaceful and fair referendum . . . under the auspices of the Organization of African Unity and the United Nations'.[34] Though the UN had not admitted the SADR to membership, its call for Morocco to enter into direct negotiations with Polisario *implied* recognition, as Zartman points out.[35] Having thus in effect pre-judged the issue to Morocco's detriment, the General Assembly had made it more difficult for the Secretariat to be accepted in Rabat as a mediator in the conflict. In this regard there are parallels to the situation in Kampuchea. Indeed, following his failure to secure support for a diluted version of the OAU peace plan during the 1985 session of the General Assembly, the Moroccan Foreign Minister told the Fourth Committee that his country would henceforth refuse to discuss 'the so-called question of Western Sahara' in any UN body. 'Good-bye, Mr. Chairman, goodbye for ever', he said.[36]

Nevertheless, the UN was not as partisan for Polisario as was the OAU, while it is clear that, like the Vietnamese and the PRK, Morocco came to make a distinction between 'the UN' and its Secretary-General. As a result, a 'good offices' mission shared by the Secretary-General and the Chairman of the OAU, called for by the General Assembly in December 1985, was accepted by Morocco as well as by Polisario in early April 1986. Algeria and Mauritania also accepted invitations from Pérez de Cuéllar to send official observers to the talks.[37] By virtue of his greater impartiality and the greater technical resources of the UN, the leading role in the joint 'good offices' mission was assumed by the UN Secretary-General, though successive OAU Chairmen were certainly not inactive. This assignment, the acceptance of which represented abandonment of the previous OAU/Polisario insistence on direct negotiations, made striking progress over the next three years.

Morocco itself had *in principle* long accepted the holding of a referendum in the Western Sahara, and in July 1986 agreed that full responsibility for its organisation and conduct should be assumed by the UN, as proposed by Pérez de Cuéllar.[38] Hassan also indicated that he would abide by the outcome of the referendum, and a year later also agreed to the despatch to the territory of a UN 'technical survey mission', the aim of which would be to gather information required by the UN and the OAU in making realistic proposals relating to the ceasefire and referendum.[39] Though the conclusions of the mission, which had conducted its work in November 1987, were kept a closely guarded secret, it had obviously not discovered any insuperable problems – despite the wide differences between the parties over *who should vote, what they should be asked to vote on*, and *under what conditions*. For at the end of May 1988, Pérez de Cuéllar, who had recently been in contact with Polisario and had also engaged in 'extremely useful, extremely important' talks with Hassan in Rabat at the beginning of the month, informed an OAU summit meeting that practical arrangements for a referendum could 'commence without difficulty'. In the interval between his visit to Rabat and the OAU summit, diplomatic relations had also been restored between Morocco and Algeria after a break of twelve years,[40] and in June King Hassan even attended a Maghreb summit in Algiers.[41] Optimism was now in the air, and was further encouraged by reports of direct talks held in Jeddah for two weeks in July between an Algerian delegation to which were attached members of Polisario and a Moroccan delegation which included a member of Hassan's family.[42]

In early August, just days after Iran finally accepted a ceasefire in the Gulf War, the Secretary-General was able to announce that, jointly with the OAU Chairman, he had put compromise proposals on a ceasefire and referendum to the parties to the Western Sahara conflict and asked for approval by 1 September.[43] Though details were not disclosed, the plan probably contained the following proposals: that, in addition to the straight choice hitherto favoured by the OAU between independence and integration into Morocco, the referendum should include a question on the desirability of Saharawi autonomy under the Moroccan crown; that Morocco should pull out between a half and three-quarters of its troops and confine the rest to barracks during the referendum; that a Special Representative should be appointed by the Secretary-General to oversee the arrangements, with the assistance of a 2000-strong UN peacekeeping force; that Polisario fighters should simultaneously retire to bases under UN supervision; and that eligibility to vote should be decided by a UN team on the basis of the 1974 Spanish census of the territory.[44]

In the middle of 1988 there was a general improvement in relations

among the countries of the Maghreb, and serious summit discussion
of rebuilding intra-regional trade and strengthening Maghreb bargaining power with the European Community by creating a common
market for the region itself. It was against this background that in the
last days of August 1988 Polisario and Moroccan officials discussed
the UN plan with Pérez de Cuéllar in Geneva, and on 30 August
agreed *in principle* to accept it. This was regarded as a major
breakthrough by Western diplomats as well as by UN officials, and
there were hopes that a formal ceasefire would be in place within one
month and that the referendum could be held within six.[45] On 20
September the Security Council endorsed the plan unanimously, and
Héctor Gros Espiell of Uruguay was appointed Special Representative for Western Sahara. This was necessary, Pérez de Cuéllar
explained to the Council, because 'the progress already made . . . is a
preliminary and favourable result, which it is extremely important to
consolidate in order to preserve the momentum of the process'.[46]

The urgency in the Secretary-General's desire to consolidate
progress was not surprising, for on 30 August both parties had
qualified their acceptance of the UN plan with 'remarks and
comments',[47] and less than a week later Polisario sought to give the
impression that the continuing refusal of Morocco to engage in direct
talks with it remained an obstacle to implementation of the plan.[48]
(Another seems to have been Polisario's determination to continue
insisting on total Moroccan withdrawal prior to the referendum.) By
December there was still no formal ceasefire. Nevertheless, at this
juncture King Hassan improved the atmosphere once again by
announcing, at last, that his palace doors were open to Polisario,
albeit for 'discussions, and not negotiations'. This prompted Polisario
to declare a unilateral truce at the end of the month pending the
talks.[49]

The first publicly admitted talks between Morocco and Polisario
duly took place in Marrakesh in early January 1989 and, though not
followed up, appear to have confirmed an *informal* ceasefire. For its
part, the UN Secretariat – assisted by Spanish experts who had
worked on the 1974 census – remained very active in preparing for
the referendum during the following months, and by May was
independently reported to have made 'considerable progress'.[50] In
the middle of 1989 implementation talks seemed still to be on course,
albeit taking much longer than had been hoped a year earlier, for on
the eve of a visit to the region by Pérez de Cuéllar in June, Polisario
announced that it would release 200 Moroccan prisoners as a gesture

of goodwill (though this was rejected by Hassan). Furthermore, shortly after the conclusion of his visit the Secretary-General announced, on 30 June, that agreement had been reached on the establishment of a 'technical mission' designed to 'facilitate and accelerate implementation of the UN–OAU settlement proposals'. This had its first meeting in New York on 12 July,[51] and simultaneously Polisario dropped its previous insistence on unconditional Moroccan troop withdrawal prior to the referendum; it also used 'unusually conciliatory language about King Hassan'.[52]

Unfortunately, after this things began to unravel. Clearly frustrated by the failure of Hassan to respond to its gestures with concessions of his own, and apparently believing that Hassan was playing for time in the expectation that broader developments in the Maghreb[53] and internal disagreements within Polisario were making the latter's position weaker, in early October Polisario launched two attacks on 'the wall'. The informal ceasefire was at an end, Hassan called off a planned second round of talks, and the prospect of a UN-supervised referendum receded.[54]

The UN had nevertheless made more progress towards settling this dispute than any other mediator in the past, and it is probably still too early to conclude that the process cannot be revived. Why had the parties to this conflict turned to the UN, and why had its intervention proved potent? First of all, in contrast with the situation in Namibia, neither of the superpowers had sufficient interest in it to make an effort themselves, and other potential mediators in the region had tried before and failed. The OAU and Algeria itself, both with traditions of mediation, were unacceptable to Morocco because they were regarded as part of the problem. Secondly, Hassan was able to save face by appearing to make concessions to the UN (which had not directly recognised the SADR) rather than to Polisario and the Algerians. Thirdly, the UN had great technical experience of the kind of problem which would have to be faced in settling a conflict of this kind. And fourthly, by 1988 the prestige of Pérez de Cuéllar had risen very considerably indeed.

CYPRUS

The conflict between the Greek majority and the Turkish minority in Cyprus has its roots in the freedom struggle of the Greeks during the period of the Ottoman empire. However, the immediate origins of the conflict lie in the 1950s when the island's colonial rulers, the British, who had acquired it from the Sublime Porte in 1878 and subsequently developed an exaggerated view of its strategic significance, stirred up Turkish apprehensions about seizure of the island by the Greek-led nationalist movement, EOKA, as part of their futile plans to cling on to it themselves. Turks in Cyprus had a dire picture painted for them of life under a government dominated by their traditional enemies, while the government in Ankara was invited to interest itself in the problem, not least because of the strategic implications for Turkey of the EOKA policy of *enosis*: union between Cyprus and Greece. (Cyprus is only forty miles from Turkey's southern coast and as recently as the early 1920s Greece had sought to conquer Constantinople and the shores of Asia Minor.) By late 1963, British bungling in Cyprus had spawned unprecedented communal hatred, an unworkable independence constitution (ostensibly guaranteed by Britain, Greece and Turkey), and a deterioration in Greek–Turkish relations to such an extent that, although nominally NATO 'allies', they were on the verge of war.

At this juncture a UN peacekeeping force (UNFICYP) was sent to the island, and this has held the ring between the two communities ever since. However, in 1974 the poise of UNFICYP was temporarily disturbed and the Cyprus problem exacerbated when, following a coup on the island which installed in power a wild, pro-*enosis* faction backed by the junta which had seized power in Athens in 1967, the Turkish army invaded.[55] With the United States unwilling to offend either of its Eastern Mediterranean allies, and Britain in consequence supine,[56] it was not long before Turkey had occupied most of the northern half of the island and thousands of Greek Cypriots were homeless. Cyprus was effectively partitioned (as the Turks had long desired) and in February 1975 the establishment of the 'Turkish Federated State of Cyprus' was announced. But this was hardly a solution satisfactory to *both* sides. Though the governments in both Athens and Nicosia were taken over by more moderate elements in the aftermath of the Turkish invasion and Britain made an energetic attempt to promote negotiations, an impasse was soon reached. For it quickly became clear that the Turks, exhilarated by their military achievement, would settle for nothing less than a federal constitution with a weak centre based on a geographical division of the island on terms which reflected their military power rather than their proportion of the island's population – a humiliation to the Greeks.[57]

Despite the failure of the talks which followed the Turkish

invasion, hopes for a negotiated solution have remained alive because it was clear even then that there was some (private) sympathy in the Greek Cypriot community for the *principle* of a bizonal federal constitution as the basis for a settlement, and subsequently there were intimations that in return for this the Turks would surrender some of the territory they had occupied in the north.[58] Moreover, personal relations between the Greek and Turkish Cypriot leaderships have sometimes been good and, although there have been arguments over the venue of negotiations, there was no problem over holding them directly until the Turkish Cypriots declared their independence in 1983. Following the failure of the British effort at mediation in the immediate aftermath of the invasion, the work was resumed by the UN Secretary-General, Kurt Waldheim, assisted by his Special Representative on the island. (The Secretariat had been involved in mediation over Cyprus since UNFICYP was created in 1964; on an intercommunal basis since June 1968.)[59]

In his memoirs Waldheim states that this new mission of good offices between the two Cypriot communities proved to be the most time-consuming and also 'the most thankless and frustrating' of all the tasks which he was called on to perform during his term of office.[60] (This is echoed by Urquhart in his memoirs.)[61] He also admits that despite all his efforts a settlement 'was not much closer when I departed than when I arrived'.[62] Nevertheless, he also claims with justice that some progress was made on 'secondary issues', such as the plight of remaining refugees, the whereabouts of missing persons, and family visits across the demarcation line, and – perhaps more importantly – that procedural and constitutional 'guidelines' had been tentatively agreed (the latter, which were of a federal nature, in early 1977) which would make a settlement easier when compromise became politically possible.[63]

However, subsequent developments made it less rather than more likely that the two sides would find compromise possible in the near future. First, the death occurred, shortly after the 1977 guidelines were agreed, of the charismatic and relatively pragmatic President of Cyprus, Archbishop Makarios. Makarios was replaced by a less secure leader, Spyros Kyprianou, who had no personal rapport with the Turkish Cypriot leader, Rauf Denktash. Secondly, there was sharp deterioration in Greek–Turkish relations which followed the coming to power in Athens of Andreas Papandreou's socialist PASOK in 1981, with its 'obsessive hostility' towards the Turks.[64] Thirdly, success rewarded the Greek Cypriot campaign to secure overwhelming support (chiefly from the Soviet bloc and the Non-Aligned Movement) for an anti-Turkish resolution in the UN General Assembly, 'the effect of which was to encourage false hopes among the Greek Cypriots and to cause a hardening of attitudes among the Turks'[65] – a classic example of the anti-diplomatic side of the United Nations. Fourthly came the declaration on 15 November 1983, which the passing of this resolution provoked, of the establishment of the Turkish Republic of Northern Cyprus (TRNC) as an independent state. And finally, of course, the shadow of the revived cold war fell unsettlingly over this regional conflict as it did over others. Turkey had the military edge on the ground, and the Reagan administration (like Nixon's in 1974) was unwilling to push it too hard towards compromise for fear of unhinging the south-eastern flank of NATO; the fact that Greece had fallen under the sway of a 'truculent' socialist government only strengthened this disinclination.[66]

Pérez de Cuéllar, as noted in Chapter 2, had himself been the Secretary-General's Special Representative in Cyprus for two years prior to his election to the head of the Secretariat. He was therefore extremely familiar with the problems of the island and realistic in his approach towards them. His own Special Representative, Hugo Gobbi of Argentina, was also credited with being a skilful and patient negotiator.[67] Nevertheless, though pressing energetically for a solution based on the widely accepted *territory in exchange for federalism* formula, plus establishment of an upper house with equal and a lower one with proportional representation, the UN continued to face a formidable task. Following separate meetings with delegations from the two sides in Vienna in August, Pérez de Cuéllar chaired proximity talks with Kyprianou and Denktash in New York in September. Then in January 1985 he staged a 'summit meeting' in New York at which he put to them an *interim* settlement proposal based on this formula and including mechanisms for the negotiation of outstanding differences, for example on the vital question of troop withdrawals. This, however, was rejected by the Greek Cypriots as too close to the favoured Turkish solution of a federation with a weak centre, and the summit collapsed. In April the Secretary-General suggested changes which allowed Kyprianou to accept the draft settlement but Denktash then insisted that this should be sent back for consideration at the lower level of officials. As a result, further proximity talks at this level were conducted in November and again in February 1986,[68] and in March Pérez de Cuéllar produced a draft 'framework agreement'. At this point he seemed to one close observer at least to be 'on the verge of success'.[69] However, though the draft once more found favour with the Turkish Cypriots it was no longer acceptable to the Greek Cypriots! Stiffened by an improved showing in elections in December and perhaps also by a Soviet proposal made in January for an international conference on Cyprus under UN auspices,[70] Kyprianou had passed up another chance to stop the drift towards the permanent division of the island. He was, however, supported in this stance by the British House of Commons Foreign Affairs Committee, among others.[71]

In a report issued in June 1986 Pérez de Cuéllar made it clear that he was not prepared to support further concessions to the Greek point of view and implicitly blamed Kyprianou for the current impasse. For the time being, as the Secretary-General admitted, the UN mediation had exhausted its alternatives.[72] And indeed, it was not until 1988 that any further progress seemed possible.

In elections at the beginning of 1988 Kyprianou, who had lost support as a result of his inflexibility in the UN negotiations, was replaced as President of Cyprus and leader of the Greek Cypriots by an independent candidate, George Vassiliou. The new President, an economist and self-made millionaire, had secured his narrow victory by virtue of 'a brilliantly organised campaign, communist backing and tactical voting'.[73] On the national question, however, there seemed initially little chance that he would prove any more flexible than Kyprianou. He had campaigned on support for the Soviet proposal for an international conference and demilitarisation of the whole island; he had also turned down the last UN formula as 'unworkable'.[74] His first public statements on the issue as President reflected if anything even more hard-line attitudes than those of his predecessor, and publicly at any rate infuriated the Turks.[75]

Nevertheless, immediately after the elections in Cyprus, Pérez de Cuéllar sent to the island a new Special Representative, Oscar Camilión, a former Argentinian foreign minister, to investigate the chances of resuming the intercommunal talks. These certainly were improving, not least because Athens was acquiring an increasingly strong card with which to trade for a Turkish withdrawal from northern Cyprus: its ability to block the closer relationship between Turkey and the European Community which had now become a major priority for Ankara. This was underlined by the assumption of the EC Presidency by Greece during the second half of 1988.[76] Just prior to the elections in Cyprus, the Turkish and Greek Prime Ministers (Ozal and Papandreou) had met at Davos in Switzerland

and pledged themselves to a process – the so-called 'Davos process' – of general rapprochement.[77] In pursuit of this, in mid-June Turgut Ozal paid a three-day visit to Athens, the first by a Turkish premier since 1952.

Other considerations seemed to favour a resumption of dialogue as well. If the initial statements of Vassiliou seemed as hardline as those of Kyprianou, at least there was a hope that the new Greek Cypriot leader, now being described as a 'pragmatist', would develop a better personal relationship with Rauf Denktash.[78] Perhaps he was also affected, as indeed he claimed to be during a visit to the United States in early August, by the 'peace epidemic' currently sweeping through the world's regional conflicts.[79] (Iran had just accepted the Security Council's call for a ceasefire in the Gulf war.) And it would not be surprising if some alarm was now being occasioned in Cyprus, especially among Greek Cypriots, by the worsening financial crisis in UNFICYP. In June 1986 the contributor governments had already served notice that they were not prepared to go on providing soldiers and policemen for this task indefinitely,[80] and recently the Swedes had withdrawn their infantry battalion in exasperation at the lack of political progress.[81]

In the light of these developments, it is not surprising that on 15 June, while Ozal was still in Athens, the Secretary-General should have reported to the Security Council that he had 'become increasingly convinced that conditions were becoming ripe to break the deadlock' and that, as a result, he proposed to launch a new initiative.[82] Following this, at a lunch with Pérez de Cuéllar in Geneva on 24 August, Vassiliou and Denktash announced their agreement to resume, without pre-conditions, direct negotiations and attempt to achieve a comprehensive settlement by 1 June 1989.[83]

Between September and March 1989 the two leaders held two rounds of exploratory talks in Nicosia under Camilión's chairmanship.[84] To no one's real surprise, these gave the lie to the euphoria of the previous August. Nevertheless, a measure of agreement seemed to have been achieved at least on the shape of a workable federal system,[85] and in his report to the Security Council on 31 May Pérez de Cuéllar said that they had 'progressed to the point where the contours of an overall agreement are discernible'. Next, after he had personally conducted two days of talks with Vassiliou and Denktash in New York, on 29 June the Secretary-General announced that they had agreed to meet him again in September and 'launch the negotiation' on the outline agreement which was emerging.[86] This appeared to be shaped by his own ideas.[87]

The June deadline had slipped but the talks still seemed to be on course[88] when an incident on 19 July on the 'Green Line' dividing the island soured the atmosphere. Denktash was already being reported as less happy with the course of the negotiations than Vassiliou,[89] and in these circumstances no further talks took place in Nicosia. In August, he flatly rejected the latest compromise proposals advocated by the UN Secretary-General,[90] who found it necessary, in the circumstances, to call off the discussions arranged for September.[91] Though in December Denktash agreed to resume negotiations under UN auspices in early 1990,[92] the chances of the 'Cyprus problem' being 'solved' by the UN or anyone else were by this time much diminished. This was because the Greek hand had been (at least temporarily) weakened by an announcement by the European Commission, in December 1989, that Turkey's application for EC membership should not be considered until at least 1993.[93] For, as Peter Loizos has emphasised, the 'Cyprus problem' has always been seen by the Turks as the physical insecurity of the Turkish Cypriot minority, and this was 'solved' to the 'relative satisfaction of most Turkish Cypriots, and of Ankara' by the occupation of the north of the island in 1974.[94] As a result, it will need *real* pressure and *real* guarantees to get them out.

THE ARAB–ISRAELI CONFLICT

The origins of this most stubborn and dangerous of all regional conflicts, rooted in the resentments of Arabs displaced from Palestine because of the Zionist belief that Jews would never be safe until they had *a state of their own*, are too well known to require elaboration here.[95] The intractability of the conflict derives chiefly from the fact that Israeli hardliners, in the ascendant for most of the time since the election to the premiership of Menachem Begin in 1977, refuse to surrender to the Palestinians, on ideological as well as security grounds, the territory which is the perennial centre-piece of settlement proposals: the West Bank of the Jordan River. Its danger lies in its location in an area of 'vital' strategic interest to the superpowers and in the fact that, while Israel is closely supported by the United States, the most radical Arab states (particularly Syria) have been supported by the Soviet Union since at least 1955.

Despite its central role in the birth of the state of Israel in 1948, the United Nations has not been at the centre of serious diplomatic attempts to grapple with this conflict or of negotiations concerned with immediate problems of military disengagement, for that matter, since the failure of the Jarring mission in 1970.[96] This is partly because of the antipathy of Israel towards the United Nations, where the hated Palestine Liberation Organisation (PLO) was granted permanent observer status in 1974. Not surprisingly, the feeling in Israel of implacable UN hostility towards it reached its deepest point with the passing of the 'Zionism is racism' resolution by the General Assembly in November of the following year.[97] Subsequently the belief has been fuelled by periodic clashes between Israeli forces and sections of the UN peacekeeping force in Lebanon (UNIFIL). Another reason for the marginalisation of the UN in Arab–Israeli diplomacy is the long-standing opposition to a major role for it on the part of the United States. This is partly a reflection of Israeli pressure, to which Washington is notoriously vulnerable, but also of a strong American determination to minimise the opportunities for Soviet intervention in the Middle East, which has generally been a higher United States priority than settling the Arab–Israeli dispute.[98]

In fact, the most serious effort to achieve a comprehensive solution to the Arab–Israeli dispute was made between 1977 and 1979 in talks between Egypt and Israel mediated by President Carter (the so-called 'Camp David talks'), which produced a peace treaty between the two major antagonists at the cost of fudging the Palestinian issue. The UN played no role in the Camp David 'peace process'.[99] Present efforts remain glued to the Camp David format, with the only difference being the desire of the Bush administration in the United States (so far ungratified) to inject some form of independent Palestinian representation into the negotiations.

Nevertheless, it would be a mistake to conclude that the United Nations has been irrelevant to Middle East diplomacy even in the comparatively recent past, and it would be injudicious to predict that it will be irrelevant in the future. The role of the Security Council in the diplomacy which followed both the Six-Day War in 1967 and the Yom Kippur War in October 1973 has already been noted in Chapter 1. The 'territory for peace' formula, expressed in Security Council resolution 242 of November 1967, has been the bedrock of all proposals for a comprehensive settlement ever since. Moreover, as even Henry Kissinger, then United States Secretary of State, acknowledges, it would have been difficult to bring Arabs and Israelis 'face to face at a high political level for the first time in a quarter of a century', after the Yom Kippur War, in the absence of Soviet–American co-chairmanship under a vague UN imprimatur in Geneva.[100] (The Geneva Conference, which took place in late December 1973, was convened by the Secretary-General and presided over by him in the 'opening phase'. This was a compromise between the Egyptians, who wanted a bigger role for the UN in order to dilute Soviet influence, and the Israelis who, for reasons already explained, wanted the UN role to be merely ceremonial.)[101] According to Kissinger, American policy in the Middle East was to move 'step-by-step' rather than try at once for a comprehensive settlement. He was also convinced that only 'an essentially bilateral diplomacy' would produce progress. Nevertheless, he regarded the Geneva Conference as valuable. Among other things, this was because it would 'symbolize trends toward making peace', preserve contact between the superpowers 'during the delicate phase while the cease-fire hung in the balance', and above all provide a 'framework' which would *legitimise* direct Arab–Israeli contacts *subsequently*. 'The Geneva Conference,' concludes Kissinger, 'whatever its bizarre aspects, . . . opened the door to peace through which later Egypt and Israel walked'.[102]

Following a joint Soviet–American attempt to revive it in 1977, the Geneva format was denounced by the Begin government as an attempt to impose a superpower settlement. It was then abandoned by the Egyptians and the Americans in favour of the Camp David format, and its re-introduction has been repeatedly rejected by the powerful Likud bloc in the Israeli parliament ever since. Nevertheless, there has remained strong support for an approach to the Arab–Israeli dispute based on the idea of a limited international conference held under UN auspices. This support revived in 1985 after the collapse of efforts to organise a joint Jordanian-PLO negotiating position made it essential for King Hussein to obtain alternative diplomatic cover, and at a time when the more conciliatory (Labour) leader, Shimon Peres, headed the Israeli coalition government. With Israel for the moment speaking kindly of the idea, the United States began to swing behind it as well, and it became a key element in the 'Shultz initiative' of early 1988. Under this proposal, the international conference would precede bilateral negotiations between Israel and a Jordanian-'Palestinian' delegation. Attending the conference, at the invitation of the UN Secretary-General, would be all of the regional 'parties' (implying the possibility of an invitation to the PLO) and the permanent members of the Security Council. They would all have to accept Security Council resolutions 242 and 338. Finally, while the negotiating parties might, by agreement, report to the conference from time to time, the conference – as earlier agreed by the Jordanians and Israel – would have no plenary powers; it would not, in other words, have any power either to impose its views or veto the results of the bilateral negotiations.[103] (This last feature was, of course, designed to allay Israeli fears.)

Unfortunately, by the time that the Shultz initiative was launched the Likud leader, Yitzhak Shamir, had taken over from Peres as head of the coalition government and predictably torpedoed the plan. Nevertheless, support continued to grow for an international conference in some form. Apart from the Soviet Union (which wanted a stronger role for the conference – and thus for itself – than was provided for in the Shultz initiative[104]), significant support also came from the EC.[105] Support in the General Assembly was overwhelming.

The main reason for this upsurge in support for the international conference approach was, of course, the Palestinian *intifadah* (uprising), which began in December 1987 and has dramatically raised the temperature of the dispute. Other recent developments have made this approach seem more plausible. These include the improvement in Soviet–Israeli relations, with Moscow expressing its interest in restoring the diplomatic relations with Israel which it severed after the Six-Day War;[106] and the more moderate posture adopted by the PLO (in December 1988 it unambiguously renounced terrorism and accepted Israel's right to exist). The implications for an international conference of the spectacular ending of Egypt's isolation in the Arab world in 1989, culminating with the restoration of relations between Cairo and Damascus, are, however, double-edged. On the one hand, the spread of moderation among the Arab states (in regard to Israel), of which Egypt's return to the fold is cause as well as effect, may make them more acceptable conferees to the Israelis and the Americans. On the other, it may give Egypt less need to seek the diplomatic cover of a UN conference in future negotiations with Israel.

With such overwhelming support for the international conference format, it seems likely that the UN is once more doomed to preside, at one point or another, over an attempt to negotiate a settlement of the Palestinian issue. This would secure the endorsement of any agreement by the Russians and the Syrians, give the Jordanians the cover they desperately need, and perhaps make it easier for Likud-niks, in the jostle and relative anonymity of such a large crowd, to sit down with the PLO, without which organisation there can be no final negotiation on the Palestinian question.

9 Conclusion

On the evidence of this and earlier studies, it seems clear that the United Nations fulfils three main diplomatic roles. It provides a convenient forum for general diplomacy (which includes intelligence gathering), it legitimises diplomacy, and it mediates. There is also little doubt that over the last few years, through the exploitation of these roles by member states and by the Secretariat, the United Nations has made a contribution of varying degrees of importance to diplomatic breakthroughs in some dangerous 'regional conflicts'. In others, it has either come close to or made significant progress towards breakthroughs of both procedural and substantive kinds. In short, the recent past, especially the *annus mirabilis* of 1988, has witnessed a productive return to the UN.

The diplomatic revival of the United Nations has been prompted by developments both inside and outside the organisation. These include the institutionalisation of 'secret diplomacy' in the Security Council, the election of an ideal Secretary-General, the positive response of the General Assembly to Western pressure for reform, and above all the thaw in US–Soviet and Sino–Soviet relations. Most of these points are obvious. However, it is also obvious that they do not provide a sufficient explanation of this remarkable return to the UN. It is now important, therefore, to consider if, in the light of recent history, the United Nations has unique attributes, or a unique combination of attributes, which place it in an unrivalled position to assist in the diplomatic settlement of acute international conflicts, as the Soviet Union now insists.

As a diplomatic forum the UN is especially significant for making possible discreet direct discussions, usually of an exploratory nature, between states (or between states and organisations such as the PLO) which have no formal relations and, as a result, either cannot afford to be *seen* talking to each other or can but, because of the absence of formal relations, do not find this easy. (The UN was an important point of contact between the United States and the MPLA government of Angola.) While the UN is one among many vehicles for encouraging underground diplomacy,[1] there is little doubt that in this regard it does possess a unique combination of assets. It has near universal membership, while heads of government and foreign ministers regularly attend the annual opening of each new session of the General Assembly in September. Moreover, the permanent missions are normally staffed by diplomats of high calibre, a fact which is by no means unconnected to the vitality and importance of the city of New York and the proximity of this city to Washington, capital of the most powerful state in the world. It might also be added here that the Chinese are believed to value the new secret meetings of the 'Big Five' because the agenda and terms of debate tend to be dominated by the more pragmatic Western powers; ideological differences with the Soviet Union can thus be either minimised or discounted altogether.[2]

There is a difference between the permanent UN missions and peripatetic statesmen of unfriendly states exploiting their legitimate proximity in New York (or some other UN venue) in order to make *discreet contact*, and the use of the UN's imprimatur in order to make it easier for hostile powers to enter *publicly admitted negotiations* and, following this, perhaps retreat from dangerous postures without losing face. This is the difference between the diplomatic forum of convenience and diplomatic legitimising functions of the UN. The operation of the latter, which has more important implications than the term 'good offices' suggests,[3] is seen most obviously in limited international conferences of the kind convened by the UN on the Middle East in Geneva in December 1973, with their avowedly 'ceremonial' roles, but is *also at work in the Security Council itself*. Indeed, the Security Council is a permanent example, and the most important of all examples, of the operation of this role. (The UN may also serve to legitimise mediation efforts conducted by others, as it did with the labours of the Western Contact Group on Namibia in the late 1970s and early 1980s.)

The United Nations is not the only body which can legitimise contact and thus provide an opportunity for bitter enemies to save face. States, a group of states in a region and regional organisations can all do this. But the UN is normally the best placed. This point is most tellingly developed by Conor Cruise O'Brien in his brilliant, rambling essay, *The United Nations: Sacred Drama*, published over twenty years ago and now usually ignored.[4] The United Nations, points out O'Brien, enacts a highly publicised drama, principally in the General Assembly but also in the Security Council and other 'theatres'. It is 'sacred' drama, he adds, less conventionally, because it originates in fear and prayer, in this case fear of and prayer addressed to man.[5] It is, in other words, at the United Nations, and only at the United Nations, *that common humanity expresses through varied and complex ritual its dedication to peace*. In addition to being a forum and a stage, therefore, the United Nations is also a shrine, and the Secretary-General is its 'high priest'.[6]

At the United Nations, then, there is an authority before which all sovereign states may kneel without loss of dignity. For the big powers, especially the superpowers, there is no other. Who else can *they* defer to? UN resolutions are especially important when they sanctify the retreat of a big power which wants to climb down from a position in which it cannot remain without serious risk of dangerous and possibly suicidal military conflict with a rival. The classic examples are Britain and France during the Suez crisis and the Soviet Union in the Cuban missiles crisis.[7] This lesson has now been reinforced by the role of the United Nations in Angola/Namibia. But by handing responsibility to the United Nations (however it chooses to deal with it) the big powers may also obtain an excuse for 'expedient but inglorious' *non-intervention*,[8] as the United States did during the Hungarian counter-revolution in 1956, the Soviet Union did in Lebanon in 1982,[9] and Britain did in Cyprus in 1974. As Brian Urquhart says, 'The Secretary-General may not be able to *solve* the problem, but at least his efforts give the pretext for resisting domestic pressures for action that might well be fatal.'[10] In short, the UN can sanctify inaction as well as retreat.

This same quality of sanctity which puts the UN in such a favourable position to legitimise negotiations between bitter enemies, also gives the Secretary-General an important advantage when he actively intervenes in a conflict, when, that is to say, he assumes the mantle of 'mediator'. In the same way that it is easier for enemies to attend a conference, *ad hoc* or permanent, at the invitation of the Secretary-General, so it is easier for them to grant concessions in negotiations at the suggestion of this 'secular Pope'[11] or one of his anointed representatives. This lesson has now been reinforced by the role of the United Nations in the Gulf War and Afghanistan. What other attributes does the UN Secretariat possess which suit it to the role of mediator, the third main diplomatic role of the world organisation?

Impartiality, of course, is not a corollary of spirituality, since this implies standards. Nevertheless, in the case of the United Nations these standards are inevitably vague and even contradictory, while greatest prominence is given to peace itself. In practice, therefore, the Secretary-General, exploiting with skill the small degree of personal latitude given to him in the UN Charter, has not found it excessively difficult to establish a *reputation for impartiality* in regional conflicts by making peace his chief, or at any rate, *first* goal. (In Afghanistan, for example, 'self-determination' was discounted in favour of reducing tensions between the superpowers.) A reputation for impartiality, though minimised by some,[12] has assisted the Secretariat in its mediating role, as Pérez de Cuéllar himself emphasises.[13] (It was while the Secretary-General was tainted by association with a hostile General Assembly or Security Council that UN mediation was resisted by Israel, the People's Republic of Kampuchea, and South Africa, and for long treated with considerable hostility by Iran.)

If UN mediation is assisted by the sanctity and impartiality of the Secretariat, it is also helped by the *continuous* attention which the Secretariat is able to devote to it. This is because it is the job of the United Nations to help states to resolve their conflicts in a peaceful manner in a way that this is not the job of states; this is not merely a normative duty but an unvarying requirement of institutional self-interest.[14] Moreover, once the Secretary-General is given a specific job of this sort to do, it is also clearly easier for his political masters routinely to renew his mandate than to bring it to an end. In contrast to the UN, states only engage in mediation when they see some positive advantage to themselves in the activity. As Touval puts it, with states chiefly in mind, 'mediators, like brokers, are in it for profit'.[15] Since most states are subject to sharper and more frequent political changes than the UN, and, even if not, sometimes find their attention to foreign affairs subjected to the demands of an electoral cycle (as in the pre-eminent case of the United States[16]), their mediation is likely to be considerably more episodic. But as all professional diplomats, since at least the time of Richelieu, have been aware, 'negotiations must always be a process rather than an episode'.[17]

The advantages of the continuity that the UN can bring to mediation, seen perhaps most obviously in the dogged and widely reviled work of Diego Cordovez in the Afghanistan negotiations, seem hitherto to have been overlooked. What are these advantages? First of all, there is familiarity, the familiarity of Secretariat personnel with the problem to hand and acquaintance with the personalities involved. Secondly, there is less publicity, which reduces the incentive to leak and also makes it less likely that false expectations will be aroused; this in turn strengthens the mediator's hand by avoiding the impression that he needs a settlement more badly than do the parties.[18]

Thirdly, there is opportunity to secure agreement on procedural issues (which, as in the Afghanistan negotiations, are sometimes substantive issues in disguise) and also on general principles of a settlement even when the time is not 'ripe' to clinch it. This makes seizing the ripe moment that much easier.[19] Of course, as Richard N. Haas has pointed out, 'diplomatic activism' when the time is unripe may be counter-productive for any number of reasons,[20] but diplomatic activism is one thing; continuous diplomatic engagement is quite another. In the Cyprus negotiations, Pérez de Cuéllar demonstrated that he was perfectly aware of this distinction. The UN, which has no electoral cycle commensurate to that of the United States to cope with, and no disintegrating empire like that of the Soviet Union to distract its attention from foreign problems, is much better placed to engage quietly in the groundwork of mediation – and then seize the moment when it arrives.

But what of the *resources* of which the UN Secretariat can dispose in order to strengthen its hand in mediating between states in dispute? Is it not true that, compared to states, especially large ones, the UN Secretariat does not have the resources (such as money and arms) which give some mediators bargaining power and sometimes even permit them to foster circumstances which are favourable to settlement?[21] This certainly was an important ingredient of Chester Crocker's success in the Angola/Namibia negotiations, as it had been with Jimmy Carter's in the Middle East earlier. In fact, the Secretariat is not without access, direct or indirect, to appropriate resources.

First, as Diego Cordovez has pointed out, the Secretary-General has the ability to mobilise resources for humanitarian relief.[22] Secondly, he can dispatch 'fact-finding' missions whose conclusions will be widely accepted, and there now seems to be more demand for these than ever. Thirdly, he derives influence from his role in the *management* of UN military and electoral observer groups and peacekeeping forces. Fourthly, he has a considerable patronage, not least ('inherited posts' notwithstanding) in the disposal of senior Secretariat posts. Fifthly, *when the Secretariat is backed by the 'Big Five' on the Security Council*, as it has been increasingly since 1987, the Secretary-General can command their military and economic resources as well – which is, of course, the whole point of Chapter VII of the Charter and the doctrine of collective security. Though the Secretariat, for obvious reasons, will never achieve any flexibility in the use of these resources, the impression of power, as well as the ever-present threat of sanctions, during a period of big power consensus, should not be underestimated. Iran probably felt something of this after the ceasefire resolution had been passed and it had been accepted by Iraq. As Pérez de Cuéllar said in his 1989 Report on the Work of the Organisation, 'Political and moral suasion, combined with a judicious use of leverage, has been the main basis of multilateral efforts aimed at the settlement of disputes'.[23] Finally, it should not be overlooked that UN mediation *backed by the 'Big Five'* carries the implicit or explicit promise of big power guarantees, perhaps the most important resource that any mediator can bring to an international dispute.

The United Nations is thus a uniquely valuable forum and legitimiser of diplomacy, and possesses assets – especially the ability to provide continuous engagement and marshall the backing of the 'Big Five' – which make it an invaluable mediator in especially intractable disputes. Member states would be well advised to give thought to how its performance in these roles, particularly the last, might be strengthened.[24] Not a bad place to start would be paying their budgetary contributions on time. (At 30 September 1989 the United States still had outstanding debts totalling $495m.)[25]

It should finally be remembered that the UN theatre has another pacific, though *not* diplomatic, role. As Conor Cruise O'Brien emphasises, it enables states to desist from dangerous actions by allowing them to let off steam instead, to engage in a 'rite of purification through anathema'. It did this for the Soviet Union after the Middle East war in 1967 and for the United States during the Hungarian crisis in 1956; it was seen in the 'annual Arab immolation of the State of Israel'.[26] Of course, the exploitation of the United Nations for crude and hysterical propaganda may also be dangerous. This is the argument that the UN is 'a dangerous place' because its propaganda exchanges exacerbate conflicts.[27] It is, however, difficult to see how this can be *more* dangerous than or even *equally* as dangerous as war. Fortunately, there is now less need to look to the UN for this contribution to peace but things might change again, and it is comforting to know that the UN can be used in this way as well.

Appendix 1 The Charter of the United Nations: Provisions on International Peace and Security

WE THE PEOPLES OF THE UNITED NATIONS determined

to save the succeeding generations from the scourge of war, which twice in our lifetime has brought untold sorrow to mankind, and

to reaffirm faith in fundamental human rights, in the dignity and worth of the human person, in the equal rights of men and women and of nations large and small, and

to establish conditions under which justice and respect for the obligations arising from treaties and other sources of international law can be maintained, and

to promote social progress and better standards of life in larger freedom, and for these ends

to practice tolerance and live together in peace with one another as good neighbours, and

to unite our strength to maintain international peace and security, and

to ensure, by the acceptance of principles and the institution of methods, that armed force shall not be used, save in the common interest, and

to employ international machinery for the promotion of the economic and social advancement of all peoples,

have resolved to combine our efforts to accomplish these aims.

Accordingly, our respective Governments, through representatives assembled in the city of San Francisco, who have exhibited their full powers found to be in good and due form, have agreed to the present Charter of the United Nations and do hereby establish an international organization to be known as the United Nations.

CHAPTER I
PURPOSES AND PRINCIPLES

Article 1

The purposes of the United Nations are:
  1. To maintain international peace and security, and to that end: to take

effective collective measures for the prevention and removal of threats to the peace, and for the suppression of acts of aggression or other breaches of the peace, and to bring about by peaceful means, and in conformity with the principles of justice and international law, adjustment or settlement of international disputes or situations which might lead to a breach of the peace;

2. To develop friendly relations among nations based on respect for the principle of equal rights and self-determination of peoples, and to take other appropriate measures to strengthen universal peace;

3. To achieve international co-operation in solving international problems of an economic, social, cultural, or humanitarian character, and in promoting and encouraging respect for human rights and for fundamental freedoms for all without distinction as to race, sex, language, or religion; and

4. To be a centre for harmonizing the actions of nations in the attainment of these common ends.

Article 2

The Organization and its Members, in pursuit of the Purposes stated in Article 1, shall act in accordance with the following Principles.

1. The Organization is based on the principle of the sovereign equality of all its Members.

2. All Members, in order to ensure to all of them the rights and benefits resulting from membership, shall fulfil in good faith the obligations assumed by them in accordance with the present Charter.

3. All Members shall settle their international disputes by peaceful means in such a manner that international peace and security, and justice, are not endangered.

4. All Members shall refrain in their international relations from the threat or use of force against the territorial integrity or political independence of any state, or in any other manner inconsistent with the Purposes of the United Nations.

5. All Members shall give the United Nations every assistance in any action it takes in accordance with the present Charter, and shall refrain from giving assistance to any state against which the United Nations is taking preventive or enforcement action.

6. The Organization shall ensure that states which are not Members of the United Nations act in accordance with these Principles so far as may be necessary for the maintenance of international peace and security.

7. Nothing contained in the present Charter shall authorize the United Nations to intervene in matters which are essentially within the domestic jurisdiction of any state or shall require the Members to submit such matters to settlement under the present Charter; but this principle shall not prejudice the application of enforcement measures under Chapter VII . . .

CHAPTER IV
THE GENERAL ASSEMBLY . . .
FUNCTIONS AND POWERS

Article 10

The General Assembly may discuss any questions or any matters within the scope of the present Charter or relating to the powers and functions of any organs provided for in the present Charter, and, except as provided in Article 12, may make recommendations to the Members of the United Nations or to the Security Council or to both on any such questions or matters.

Article 11

1. The General Assembly may consider the general principles of co-operation in the maintenance of international peace and security, including the principles governing disarmament and the regulation of armaments, and may make recommendations with regard to such principles to the Members or to the Security Council or to both.

2. The General Assembly may discuss any questions relating to the maintenance of international peace and security brought before it by any Member of the United Nations, or by the Security Council, or by a state which is not a Member of the United Nations in accordance with Article 35, paragraph 2, and, except as provided in Article 12, may make recommendations with regard to any such questions to the state or states concerned or to the Security Council or to both. Any such question on which action is necessary shall be referred to the Security Council by the General Assembly either before or after discussion.

3. The General Assembly may call the attention of the Security Council to situations which are likely to endanger international peace and security.

4. The powers of the General Assembly set forth in this Article shall not limit the general scope of Article 10.

Article 12

1. While the Security Council is exercising in respect of any dispute or situation the functions assigned to it in the present Charter, the General Assembly shall not make any recommendations with regard to that dispute or situation unless the Security Council so requests.

2. The Secretary-General, with the consent of the Security Council, shall notify the General Assembly at each session of any matters relative to the maintenance of international peace and security which are being dealt with by the Security Council and shall similarly notify the General Assembly, or the Members of the United Nations if the General Assembly is not in session, immediately the Security Council ceases to deal with such matters.

Article 13

1. The General Assembly shall initiate studies and make recommendations for the purpose of:
   a. promoting international co-operation in the political field and encouraging the progressive development of international law and its codification;
   b. promoting international co-operation in the economic, social, cultural, educational, and health fields, and assisting in the realization of human rights and fundamental freedoms for all without distinction as to race, sex, language, or religion.

2. The further responsibilities, functions and powers of the General Assembly with respect to matters mentioned in paragraph 1(b) above are set forth in Chapters IX and X.

Article 14

Subject to the provisions of Article 12, the General Assembly may recommend measures for the peaceful adjustment of any situation, regardless of origin, which it deems likely to impair the general welfare or friendly relations among nations, including situations resulting from a violation of the provisions of the present Charter setting forth the Purposes and Principles of the United Nations.

Article 15

1. The General Assembly shall receive and consider annual and special reports from the Security Council; these reports shall include an account of the measures that the Security Council has decided upon or taken to maintain international peace and security.

2. The General Assembly shall receive and consider reports from the other organs of the United Nations . . .

VOTING

Article 18

1. Each member of the General Assembly shall have one vote.

2. Decisions of the General Assembly on important questions shall be made by a two-thirds majority of the members present and voting. These questions shall include: recommendations with respect to the maintenance of international peace and security, the election of the non-permanent members of the Security Council, the election of the members of the Economic and Social Council, the election of members of the Trusteeship Council in accordance with paragraph 1(c) of Article 86, the admission of new Members to the United Nations, the suspension of the rights and privileges of

membership, the expulsion of Members, questions relating to the operation of the trusteeship system, and budgetary questions.

3. Decisions on other questions, including the determination of additional categories of questions to be decided by a two-thirds majority, shall be made by a majority of the members present and voting.

Article 19

A Member of the United Nations which is in arrears in the payment of its financial contributions to the Organization shall have no vote in the General Assembly if the amount of its arrears equals or exceeds the amount of the contributions due from it for the preceding two full years. The General Assembly may, nevertheless, permit such a member to vote if it is satisfied that the failure to pay is due to conditions beyond the control of the Member.

PROCEDURE

Article 20

The General Assembly shall meet in regular annual sessions and in such special sessions as occasion may require. Special sessions shall be convoked by the Secretary-General at the request of the Security Council or of a majority of the Members of the United Nations.

Article 21

The General Assembly shall adopt its own rules of procedure. It shall elect its President for each session.

Article 22

The General Assembly may establish such subsidiary organs as it deems necessary for the performance of its functions.

CHAPTER V
THE SECURITY COUNCIL
COMPOSITION

Article 23

1. The Security Council shall consist of fifteen Members of the United Nations. The Republic of China, France, the Union of Soviet Socialist Republics, the United Kingdom of Great Britain and Northern Ireland, and the United States of America shall be permanent members of the Security

Council. The General Assembly shall elect ten other Members of the United Nations to be non-permanent members of the Security Council, due regard being specially paid, in the first instance to the contribution of Members of the United Nations to the maintenance of international peace and security and to the other purposes of the Organization, and also to equitable geographical distribution.

2. The non-permanent members of the Security Council shall be elected for a term of two years. In the first election of the non-permanent members after the increase of the membership of the Security Council from eleven to fifteen, two of the four additional members shall be chosen for a term of one year. A retiring member shall not be eligible for immediate re-election.

3. Each member of the Security Council shall have one representative.

FUNCTIONS AND POWERS

Article 24

1. In order to ensure prompt and effective action by the United Nations, its Members confer on the Security Council primary responsibility for the maintenance of international peace and security, and agree that in carrying out its duties under this responsibility the Security Council acts on their behalf.

2. In discharging these duties the Security Council shall act in accordance with the Purposes and Principles of the United Nations. The specific powers granted to the Security Council for the discharge of these duties are laid down in Chapters VI, VII, VIII, and XII.

3. The Security Council shall submit annual and, when necessary, special reports to the General Assembly for its consideration.

Article 25

The Members of the United Nations agree to accept and carry out the decisions of the Security Council in accordance with the present Charter.

Article 26

In order to promote the establishment and maintenance of international peace and security with the least diversion for armaments of the world's human and economic resources, the Security Council shall be responsible for formulating, with the assistance of the Military Staff Committee referred to in Article 47, plans to be submitted to the Members of the United Nations for the establishment of a system for the regulation of armaments.

VOTING

Article 27

1. Each member of the Security Council shall have one vote.
2. Decisions of the Security Council on procedural matters shall be made by an affirmative vote of nine members.
3. Decisions of the Security Council on all other matters shall be made by an affirmative vote of nine members including the concurring votes of the permanent members; provided that, in decisions under Chapter VI, and under paragraph 3 of Article 52, a party to a dispute shall abstain from voting.

PROCEDURE

Article 28

1. The Security Council shall be so organized as to be able to function continuously. Each member of the Security Council shall for this purpose be represented at all times at the seat of the Organization.
2. The Security Council shall hold periodic meetings at which each of its members may, if it so desires, be represented by a member of the government or by some other specially designated representative.
3. The Security Council may hold meetings at such places other than the seat of the Organization as in its judgment will best facilitate its work.

Article 29

The Security Council may establish such subsidiary organs as it deems necessary for the performance of its functions.

Article 30

The Security Council shall adopt its own rules of procedure including the method of selecting its President.

Article 31

Any Member of the United Nations which is not a member of the Security Council may participate, without vote, in the discussion of any question brought before the Security Council whenever the latter considers that the interests of that Member are specially affected.

Article 32

Any Member of the United Nations which is not a member of the Security

Council or any state which is not a Member of the United Nations, if it is a party to a dispute under consideration by the Security Council, shall be invited to participate, without vote, in the discussion relating to the dispute. The Security Council shall lay down such conditions as it deems just for the participation of a state which is not a Member of the United Nations.

CHAPTER VI
PACIFIC SETTLEMENT OF DISPUTES

Article 33

1. The parties to any dispute, the continuance of which is likely to endanger the maintenance of international peace and security, shall, first of all, seek a solution by negotiation, enquiry, mediation, conciliation, arbitration, judicial settlement, resort to regional agencies or arrangements, or other peaceful means of their own choice.
2. The Security Council shall, when it deems necessary, call upon the parties to settle their dispute by such means.

Article 34

The Security Council may investigate any dispute, or any situation which might lead to international friction or give rise to a dispute, in order to determine whether the continuance of the dispute or situation is likely to endanger the maintenance of international peace and security.

Article 35

1. Any Member of the United Nations may bring any dispute, or any situation of the nature referred to in Article 34, to the attention of the Security Council or of the General Assembly.
2. A state which is not a Member of the United Nations may bring to the attention of the Security Council or of the General Assembly any dispute to which it is a party if it accepts, in advance, for the purposes of the dispute, the obligations of pacific settlement provided in the present Charter.
3. The proceedings of the General Assembly in respect of matters brought to its attention under this Article will be subject to the provisions of Articles 11 and 12.

Article 36

1. The Security Council may, at any stage of a dispute of the nature referred to in Article 33 or of a situation of like nature, recommend appropriate procedures or methods of adjustment.
2. The Security Council should take into consideration any procedures for

the settlement of the dispute which have already been adopted by the parties.

3. In making recommendations under this Article the Security Council should also take into consideration that legal disputes should as a general rule be referred by the parties to the International Court of Justice in accordance with the provisions of the Statute of the Court.

Article 37

1. Should the parties to a dispute of the nature referred to in Article 33 fail to settle it by the means indicated in that Article, they shall refer it to the Security Council.

2. If the Security Council deems that the continuance of the dispute is in fact likely to endanger the maintenance of international peace and security, it shall decide whether to take action under Article 36 or to recommend such terms of settlement as it may consider appropriate.

Article 38

Without prejudice to the provisions of Articles 33 to 37, the Security Council may, if all the parties to any dispute so request, make recommendations to the parties with a view to a pacific settlement of the dispute.

CHAPTER VII
ACTION WITH RESPECT TO THREATS TO THE PEACE, BREACHES OF THE PEACE, AND ACTS OF AGGRESSION

Article 39

The Security Council shall determine the existence of any threat to the peace, breach of the peace, or act of aggression and shall make recommendations, or decide what measures shall be taken in accordance with Articles 41 and 42, to maintain or restore international peace and security.

Article 40

In order to prevent an aggravation of the situation, the Security Council may, before making the recommendations or deciding upon the measures provided for in Article 39, call upon the parties concerned to comply with such provisional measures as it deems necessary or desirable. Such provisional measures shall be without prejudice to the rights, claims, or position of the parties concerned. The Security Council shall duly take account of failure to comply with such provisional measures.

Article 41

The Security Council may decide what measures not involving the use of armed force are to be employed to give effect to its decisions, and it may call upon the Members of the United Nations to apply such measures. These may include complete or partial interruption of economic relations and of rail, sea, air, postal, telegraphic, radio, and other means of communication, and the severance of diplomatic relations.

Article 42

Should the Security Council consider that measures provided for in Article 41 would be inadequate or have proved to be inadequate, it may take such action by air, sea, or land forces as may be necessary to maintain or restore international peace and security. Such action may include demonstrations, blockade, and other operations by air, sea, or land forces of Members of the United Nations.

Article 43

1. All Members of the United Nations, in order to contribute to the maintenance of international peace and security, undertake to make available to the Security Council, on its call and in accordance with a special agreement or agreements, armed forces, assistance and facilities, including rights of passage, necessary for the purpose of maintaining international peace and security.
2. Such agreement or agreements shall govern the numbers and types of forces, their degree of readiness and general location, and the nature of the facilities and assistance to be provided.
3. The agreement or agreements shall be negotiated as soon as possible on the initiative of the Security Council. They shall be concluded between the Security Council and Members or between the Security Council and groups of Members and shall be subject to ratification by the signatory states in accordance with their respective constitutional processes.

Article 44

When the Security Council has decided to use force it shall, before calling upon a Member not represented on it to provide armed forces in fulfilment of the obligations assumed under Article 43, invite that Member, if the Member so desires, to participate in the decisions of the Security Council concerning the employment of contingents of that Member's armed forces.

Article 45

In order to enable the United Nations to take urgent military measures, Members shall hold immediately available national air-force contingents for combined international enforcement action. The strength and degree of readiness of these contingents and plans for their combined action shall be determined, within the limits laid down in the special agreement or agreements referred to in Article 43, by the Security Council with the assistance of the Military Staff Committee.

Article 46

Plans for the application of armed force shall be made by the Security Council with the assistance of the Military Staff Committee.

Article 47

1. There shall be established a Military Staff Committee to advise and assist the Security Council on all questions relating to the Security Council's military requirements for the maintenance of international peace and security, the employment and command of forces placed at its disposal, the regulation of armaments, and possible disarmament.

2. The Military Staff Committee shall consist of the Chiefs of Staff of the permanent members of the Security Council or their representatives. Any Member of the United Nations not permanently represented on the Committee shall be invited by the Committee to be associated with it when the efficient discharge of the Committee's responsibilities requires the participation of that Member in its work.

3. The Military Staff Committee shall be responsible under the Security Council for the strategic direction of any armed forces placed at the disposal of the Security Council. Questions relating to the command of such forces shall be worked out subsequently.

4. The Military Staff Committee, with the authorization of the Security Council and after consultation with appropriate regional agencies, may establish regional sub-committees.

Article 48

1. The action required to carry out the decisions of the Security Council for the maintenance of international peace and security shall be taken by all the Members of the United Nations or by some of them, as the Security Council may determine.

2. Such decisions shall be carried out by the Members of the United Nations directly and through their action in the appropriate international agencies of which they are members.

Article 49

The Members of the United Nations shall join in affording mutual assistance in carrying out the measures decided upon by the Security Council.

Article 50

If preventive or enforcement measures against any state are taken by the Security Council, any other state, whether a Member of the United Nations or not, which finds itself confronted with special economic problems arising from the carrying out of those measures shall have the right to consult the Security Council with regard to a solution of those problems.

Article 51

Nothing in the present Charter shall impair the inherent right of individual or collective self-defence if an armed attack occurs against a Member of the United Nations, until the Security Council has taken measures necessary to maintain international peace and security. Measures taken by members in the exercise of this right of self-defence shall be immediately reported to the Security Council and shall not in any way affect the authority and responsibility of the Security Council under the present Charter to take at any time such action as it deems necessary in order to maintain or restore international peace and security.

CHAPTER VIII
REGIONAL ARRANGEMENTS

Article 52

1. Nothing in the present Charter precludes the existence of regional arrangements or agencies for dealing with such matters relating to the maintenance of international peace and security as are appropriate for regional action, provided that such arrangements or agencies and their activities are consistent with the Purposes and Principles of the United Nations.
2. The Members of the United Nations entering into such arrangements or constituting such agencies shall make every effort to achieve pacific settlement of local disputes through such regional arrangements or by such regional agencies before referring them to the Security Council.
3. The Security Council shall encourage the development of pacific settlement of local disputes through such regional arrangements or by such regional agencies either on the initiative of the states concerned or by reference from the Security Council.
4. This Article in no way impairs the application of Articles 34 and 35.

Article 53

1. The Security Council shall, where appropriate, utilize such regional arrangements or agencies for enforcement action under its authority. But no enforcement action shall be taken under regional arrangements or by

regional agencies without the authorization of the Security Council, with the exception of measures against any enemy state, as defined in paragraph 2 of this Article, provided for pursuant to Article 107 or in regional arrangements directed against renewal of aggressive policy on the part of any such state, until such time as the Organization may, on request of the Governments concerned, be charged with the responsibility for preventing further aggression by such a state.

2. The term enemy state as used in paragraph 1 of this Article applies to any state which during the Second World War has been an enemy of any signatory of the present Charter.

Article 54

The Security Council shall at all times be kept fully informed of activities undertaken or in contemplation under regional arrangements or by regional agencies for the maintenance of international peace and security . . .

CHAPTER XV
THE SECRETARIAT

Article 97

The Secretariat shall comprise a Secretary-General and such staff as the organization may require. The Secretary-General shall be appointed by the General Assembly upon the recommendation of the Security Council. He shall be the chief administrative officer of the Organization.

Article 98

The Secretary-General shall act in that capacity in all meetings of the General Assembly, of the Security Council, of the Economic and Social Council, and of the Trusteeship Council, and shall perform such other functions as are entrusted to him by these organs. The Secretary-General shall make an annual report to the General Assembly on the work of the Organization.

Article 99

The Secretary-General may bring to the attention of the Security Council any matter which in his opinion may threaten the maintenance of international peace and security.

Article 100

1. In the performance of their duties the Secretary-General and the staff shall not seek or receive instructions from any government or from any other

authority external to the Organization. They shall refrain from any action which might reflect on their position as international officials responsible only to the Organization.

2. Each member of the United Nations undertakes to respect the exclusively international character of the responsibilities of the Secretary-General and the staff and not to seek to influence them in the discharge of their responsibilities.

Article 101

1. The staff shall be appointed by the Secretary-General under regulations established by the General Assembly.

2. Appropriate staffs shall be permanently assigned to the Economic and Social Council, the Trusteeship Council, and, as required, to other organs of the United Nations. These staffs shall form a part of the Secretariat.

3. The paramount consideration in the employment of the staff and in the determination of the conditions of service shall be the necessity of securing the highest standards of efficiency, competence, and integrity. Due regard shall be paid to the importance of recruiting the staff on as wide a geographical basis as possible.

CHAPTER XVI
MISCELLANEOUS PROVISIONS

Article 102

1. Every treaty and every international agreement entered into by any Member of the United Nations after the present Charter comes into force shall as soon as possible be registered with the Secretariat and published by it.

2. No party to any such treaty or international agreement which has not been registered in accordance with the provisions of paragraph 1 of this Article may invoke that treaty or agreement before any organ of the United Nations.

Article 103

In the event of a conflict between the obligations of the Members of the United Nations under the present Charter and their obligations under any other international agreement, their obligations under the present Charter shall prevail.

Article 104

The Organization shall enjoy in the territory of each of its Members such legal capacity as may be necessary for the exercise of its functions and the fulfilment of its purposes.

Article 105

1. The Organization shall enjoy in the territory of each of its Members such privileges and immunities as are necessary for the fulfilment of its purposes.

2. Representatives of the Members of the United Nations and officials of the Organization shall similarly enjoy such privileges and immunities as are necessary for the independent exercise of their functions in connexion with the Organization.

3. The General Assembly may make recommendations with a view to determining the details of the application of paragraphs 1 and 2 of this Article or may propose conventions to the Members of the United Nations for this purpose . . .

CHAPTER XVIII
AMENDMENTS

Article 108

Amendments to the present Charter shall come into force for all Members of the United Nations when they have been adopted by a vote of two thirds of the members of the General Assembly and ratified in accordance with their respective constitutional processes by two thirds of the Members of the United Nations, including all the permanent members of the Security Council.

Article 109

1. A General Conference of the Members of the United Nations for the purpose of reviewing the present Charter may be held at a date and place to be fixed by a two-thirds vote of the members of the General Assembly and by a vote of any nine members of the Security Council. Each Member of the United Nations shall have one vote in the conference.

2. Any alteration of the present Charter recommended by a two-thirds vote of the conference shall take effect when ratified in accordance with their respective constitutional processes by two-thirds of the Members of the United Nations including all the permanent members of the Security Council.

3. If such a conference has not been held before the tenth annual session of the General Assembly following the coming into force of the present Charter, the proposal to call such a conference shall be placed on the agenda of that session of the General Assembly, and the conference shall be held if so decided by a majority vote of the members of the General Assembly and by a vote of any seven members of the Security Council . . .

Appendix 2　Provisional Rules of Procedure of the Security Council, as Amended 21 December 1982

CHAPTER I
MEETINGS

Rule 1

Meetings of the Security Council shall, with the exception of the periodic meetings referred to in rule 4, be held at the call of the President at any time he deems necessary, but the interval between meetings shall not exceed fourteen days.

Rule 2

The President shall call a meeting of the Security Council at the request of any member of the Security Council.

Rule 3

The President shall call a meeting of the Security Council if a dispute or situation is brought to the attention of the Security Council under Article 35 or under Article 11 (3) of the Charter, or if the General Assembly makes recommendations or refers any question to the Security Council under Article 11 (2), or if the Secretary-General brings to the attention of the Security Council any matter under Article 99.

Rule 4

Periodic meetings of the Security Council called for in Article 28 (2) of the Charter shall be held twice a year, at such times as the Security Council may decide.

Rule 5

Meetings of the Security Council shall normally be held at the seat of the United Nations.

Any member of the Security Council or the Secretary-General may propose that the Security Council should meet at another place. Should the Security Council accept any such proposal, it shall decide upon the place, and the period during which the Council shall meet at such place.

CHAPTER II
AGENDA

Rule 6

The Secretary-General shall immediately bring to the attention of all representatives on the Security Council all communications from states, organs of the United Nations, or the Secretary-General concerning any matter for the consideration of the Security Council in accordance with the provisions of the Charter.

Rule 7

The provisional agenda for each meeting of the Security Council shall be drawn up by the Secretary-General and approved by the President of the Security Council.

Only items which have been brought to the attention of the representatives on the Security Council in accordance with rule 6, items covered by rule 10, or matters which the Security Council has previously decided to defer, may be included in the provisional agenda.

Rule 8

The provisional agenda for a meeting shall be communicated by the Secretary-General to the representatives on the Security Council at least three days before the meeting, but in urgent circumstances it may be communicated simultaneously with the notice of the meeting.

Rule 9

The first item of the provisional agenda for each meeting of the Security Council shall be the adoption of the agenda.

Rule 10

Any item of the agenda of a meeting of the Security Council, consideration of which has not been completed at that meeting, shall, unless the Security

Council otherwise decides, automatically be included in the agenda of the next meeting.

Rule 11

The Secretary-General shall communicate each week to the representatives on the Security Council a summary statement of matters of which the Security Council is seized and of the stage reached in their consideration.

Rule 12

The provisional agenda for each periodic meeting shall be circulated to the members of the Security Council at least twenty-one days before the opening of the meeting. Any subsequent change in or addition to the provisional agenda shall be brought to the notice of the members at least five days before the meeting. The Security Council may, however, in urgent circumstances, make additions to the agenda at any time during a periodic meeting.

The provisions of rule 7, paragraph 1, and of rule 9, shall apply also to periodic meetings.

CHAPTER III
REPRESENTATION AND CREDENTIALS

Rule 13

Each member of the Security Council shall be represented at the meetings of the Security Council by an accredited representative. The credentials of a representative on the Security Council shall be communicated to the Secretary-General not less than twenty-four hours before he takes his seat on the Security Council. The credentials shall be issued either by the Head of the State or of the Government concerned or by its Minister of Foreign Affairs. The head of Government or Minister of Foreign Affairs of each member of the Security Council shall be entitled to sit on the Security Council without submitting credentials.

Rule 14

Any member of the United Nations not a member of the Security Council and any state not a member of the United Nations, if invited to participate in a meeting or meetings of the Security Council, shall submit credentials for the representative appointed by it for this purpose. The credentials of such a representative shall be communicated to the Secretary-General not less than twenty-four hours before the first meeting which he is invited to attend.

Rule 15

The credentials of representatives on the Security Council and of any representative appointed in accordance with rule 14 shall be examined by the Secretary-General who shall submit a report to the Security Council for approval.

Rule 16

Pending the approval of the credentials of a representative on the Security Council in accordance with rule 15, such representative shall be seated provisionally with the same rights as other representatives.

Rule 17

Any representative on the Security Council, to whose credentials objection has been made within the Security Council, shall continue to sit with the same rights as other representatives until the Security Council has decided the matter.

CHAPTER IV
PRESIDENCY

Rule 18

The presidency of the Security Council shall be held in turn by the members of the Security Council in the English alphabetical order of their names. Each President shall hold office for one calendar month.

Rule 19

The President shall preside over the meetings of the Security Council and, under the authority of the Security Council, shall represent it in its capacity as an organ of the United Nations.

Rule 20

Whenever the President of the Security Council deems that for the proper fulfilment of the responsibilities of the presidency he should not preside over the Council during the consideration of a particular question with which the member he represents is directly connected, he shall indicate his decision to the Council. The presidential chair shall then devolve, for the purpose of the consideration of that question, on the representative of the member next in

English alphabetical order, it being understood that the provisions of this rule shall apply to the representatives on the Security Council called upon successively to preside. This rule shall not affect the representative capacity of the President as stated in rule 19, or his duties under rule 7.

CHAPTER V
SECRETARIAT

Rule 21

The Secretary-General shall act in that capacity in all meetings of the Security Council. The Secretary-General may authorize a deputy to act in his place at meetings of the Security Council.

Rule 22

The Secretary-General, or his deputy acting on his behalf, may make either oral or written statements to the Security Council concerning any questions under consideration by it.

Rule 23

The Secretary-General may be appointed by the Security Council, in accordance with rule 28, as rapporteur for a specified question.

Rule 24

The Secretary-General shall provide the staff required by the Security Council. This staff shall form a part of the Secretariat.

Rule 25

The Secretary-General shall give to representatives on the Security Council notice of meetings of the Security Council and of its commissions and committees.

Rule 26

The Secretary-General shall be responsible for the preparation of documents required by the Security Council and shall, except in urgent circumstances, distribute them at least forty-eight hours in advance of the meeting at which they are to be considered.

CHAPTER VI
CONDUCT OF BUSINESS

Rule 27

The President shall call upon representatives in the order in which they signify their desire to speak.

Rule 28

The Security Council may appoint a commission or committee or a rapporteur for a specified question.

Rule 29

The President may accord precedence to any rapporteur appointed by the Security Council.

The chairman of a commission or committee, or the rapporteur appointed by the commission or committee to present its report, may be accorded precedence for the purpose of explaining the report.

Rule 30

If a representative raises a point of order, the President shall immediately state his ruling. If it is challenged, the President shall submit his ruling to the Security Council for immediate decision and it shall stand unless overruled.

Rule 31

Proposed resolutions, amendments and substantive motions shall normally be placed before the representatives in writing.

Rule 32

Principal motions and draft resolutions shall have precedence in the order of their submission.

Parts of a motion or of a draft resolution shall be voted on separately at the request of any representative, unless the original mover objects.

Rule 33

The following motions shall have precedence in the order named over all principal motions and draft resolutions relative to the subject before the meeting:

1. To suspend the meeting;
2. To adjourn the meeting;
3. To adjourn the meeting to a certain day or hour;
4. To refer any matter to a committee, to the Secretary-General or to a rapporteur;
5. To postpone discussion of the question to a certain day or indefinitely; or
6. To introduce an amendment.

Any motion for the suspension or for the simple adjournment of the meeting shall be decided without debate.

Rule 34

It shall not be necessary for any motion or draft resolution proposed by a representative on the Security Council to be seconded before being put to a vote.

Rule 35

A motion or draft resolution can at any time be withdrawn so long as no vote has been taken with respect to it.

If the motion or draft resolution has been seconded, the representative on the Security Council who has seconded it may require that it be put to the vote as his motion or draft resolution with the same right of precedence as if the original mover had not withdrawn it.

Rule 36

If two or more amendments to a motion or draft resolution are proposed, the President shall rule on the order in which they are to be voted upon. Ordinarily, the Security Council shall first vote on the amendment furthest removed in substance from the original proposal and then on the amendment next furthest removed until all amendments have been put to the vote, but when an amendment adds to or deletes from the text of a motion or draft resolution, that amendment shall be voted on first.

Rule 37

Any Member of the United Nations which is not a member of the Security Council may be invited, as the result of a decision of the Security Council to participate, without vote, in the discussion of any question brought before the Security Council when the Security Council considers that the interests of that Member are specially affected, or when a Member brings a matter to the attention of the Security Council in accordance with Article 35 (1) of the Charter.

Rule 38

Any Member of the United Nations invited in accordance with the preceding rule, or in application of Article 32 of the Charter, to participate in the discussions of the Security Council may submit proposals and draft resolutions. These proposals and draft resolutions may be put to a vote only at the request of a representative on the Security Council.

Rule 39

The Security Council may invite members of the Secretariat or other persons, whom it considers competent for the purpose, to supply it with information or to give other assistance in examining matters within its competence.

CHAPTER VII
VOTING

Rule 40

Voting in the Security Council shall be in accordance with the relevant Articles of the Charter and of the Statute of the International Court of Justice.

CHAPTER VIII
LANGUAGES

Rule 41

Arabic, Chinese, English, French, Russian and Spanish shall be both the official and the working languages of the Security Council.

Rule 42

Speeches made in any of the six languages of the Security Council shall be interpreted into the other five languages.

Rule 43

(Deleted)

Rule 44

Any representative may make a speech in a language other than the languages of the Security Council. In this case, he shall himself provide for interpretation into one of those languages. Interpretation into the other languages of the Security Council by the interpreters of the Secretariat may be based on the interpretation given in the first such language.

Rule 45

Verbatim records of meetings of the Security Council shall be drawn up in the languages of the Council.

Rule 46

All resolutions and other documents shall be published in the languages of the Security Council.

Rule 47

Documents of the Security Council shall, if the Security Council so decides, be published in any language other than the languages of the Council.

CHAPTER IX
PUBLICITY OF MEETINGS, RECORDS

Rule 48

Unless it decides otherwise, the Security Council shall meet in public. Any recommendation to the General Assembly regarding the appointment of the Secretary-General shall be discussed and decided at a private meeting.

Rule 49

Subject to the provisions of rule 51, the verbatim record of each meeting of the Security Council shall be made available to the representatives on the Security Council and to the representatives of any other States which have participated in the meeting not later than 10 a.m. of the first working day following the meeting.

Rule 50

The representatives of the States which have participated in the meeting shall, within two working days after the time indicated in rule 49, inform the Secretary-General of any corrections they wish to have made in the verbatim record.

Rule 51

The Security Council may decide that for a private meeting the record shall be made in a single copy alone. This record shall be kept by the Secretary-General. The representatives of the States which have participated in the meeting shall, within a period of ten days, inform the Secretary-General of any corrections they wish to have made in this record.

Rule 52

Corrections that have been requested shall be considered approved unless the President is of the opinion that they are sufficiently important to be submitted to the representatives on the Security Council. In the latter case, the representatives on the Security Council shall submit within two working days any comments they may wish to make. In the absence of objections in this period of time, the record shall be corrected as requested.

Rule 53

The verbatim record referred to in rule 49 or the record referred to in rule 51, in which no corrections have been requested in the period of time required by rules 50 and 51, respectively, or which has been corrected in accordance with the provisions of rule 52, shall be considered as approved. It shall be signed by the President and shall become the official record of the Security Council.

Rule 54

The official record of public meetings of the Security Council, as well as the documents annexed thereto, shall be published in the official languages as soon as possible.

Rule 55

At the close of each private meeting the Security Council shall issue a *communiqué* through the Secretary-General.

Rule 56

The representatives of the members of the United Nations which have taken part in a private meeting shall at all times have the right to consult the record of that meeting in the office of the Secretary-General. The Security Council may at any time grant access to this record to authorized representatives of other Members of the United Nations.

Rule 57

The Secretary-General shall, once each year, submit to the Security Council a list of the records and documents which up to that time have been considered confidential. The Security Council shall decide which of these shall be made available to other Members of the United Nations, which shall be made public, and which shall continue to remain confidential.

CHAPTER X
ADMISSION OF NEW MEMBERS

Rule 58

Any State which desires to become a Member of the United Nations shall submit an application to the Secretary-General. This application shall contain a declaration made in a formal instrument that it accepts the obligations contained in the Charter.

Rule 59

The Secretary-General shall immediately place the application for membership before the representatives on the Security Council. Unless the Security Council decides otherwise, the application shall be referred by the President to a committee of the Security Council upon which each member of the Security Council shall be represented. The committee shall examine any application referred to it and report its conclusions thereon to the Council not less than thirty-five days in advance of a regular session of the General Assembly or, if a special session of the General Assembly is called, not less than fourteen days in advance of such session.

Rule 60

The Security Council shall decide whether in its judgment the applicant is a peace-loving State and is able and willing to carry out the obligations contained in the Charter and, accordingly, whether to recommend the applicant State for membership.

If the Security Council recommends the applicant State for membership, it shall forward to the General Assembly the recommendation with a complete record of the discussion.

If the Security Council does not recommend the applicant State for membership or postpones the consideration of the application, it shall submit a special report to the General Assembly with a complete record of the discussion.

In order to ensure the consideration of its recommendation at the next session of the General Assembly following the receipt of the application, the Security Council shall make its recommendation not less than twenty-five days in advance of a regular session of the General Assembly, nor less than four days in advance of a special session.

In special circumstances, the Security Council may decide to make a recommendation to the General Assembly concerning an application for membership subsequent to the expiration of the time limits set forth in the preceding paragraph.

CHAPTER XI
RELATIONS WITH OTHER UNITED NATIONS ORGANS

Rule 61

Any meeting of the Security Council held in pursuance of the Statute of the International Court of Justice for the purpose of the election of members of the court shall continue until as many candidates as are required for all the seats to be filled have obtained in one or more ballots an absolute majority of votes.

APPENDIX
PROVISIONAL PROCEDURE FOR DEALING WITH COMMUNICATIONS FROM PRIVATE INDIVIDUALS AND NON-GOVERNMENTAL BODIES

A. A list of all communications from private individuals and non-governmental bodies relating to matters of which the Security Council is seized shall be circulated to all representatives on the Security Council.

B. A copy of any communication on the list shall be given by the Secretariat to any representative on the Security Council at his request.

SOURCE: UN Doc. S/96/Rev.7.

Appendix 3 The Membership of the Security Council, 1987–90

1987	1988	1989	1990
Argentina	Algeria	Algeria	Canada
Bulgaria	Argentina	Brazil	*China*
China	Brazil	Canada	Colombia
Congo	*China*	*China*	Cuba
France	*France*	Colombia	Ethiopia
West Germany	West Germany	Ethiopia	Finland
Ghana	Italy	Finland	*France*
Italy	Japan	*France*	Ivory Coast
Japan	Nepal	Malaysia	Malaysia
USSR	Senegal	Nepal	Romania
United Arab	*USSR*	Senegal	South Yemen
Emirates	*UK*	*USSR*	*USSR*
UK	*USA*	*UK*	*UK*
USA	Yugoslavia	*USA*	*USA*
Venezuela	Zambia	Yugoslavia	Zaire
Zambia			

NOTE: italicized states are permanent members; the 'non-permanent' members, elected on a regional basis, hold their seats for two years.

Appendix 4 UN Security Council Resolution 598 (Gulf War Ceasefire), July 1987

The Security Council,

Reaffirming its resolution 582 (1986),

Deeply concerned that, despite its calls for a cease-fire, the conflict between the Islamic Republic of Iran and Iraq continues unabated, with further heavy loss of human life and material destruction,

Deploring the initiation and continuation of the conflict,

Deploring also the bombing of purely civilian population centres, attacks on neutral shipping or civilian aircraft, the violation of international humanitarian law and other laws of armed conflict, and, in particular, the use of chemical weapons contrary to obligations under the 1925 Geneva Protocol,

Deeply concerned that further escalation and widening of the conflict may take place,

Determined to bring to an end all military actions between Iran and Iraq,

Convinced that a comprehensive, just, honourable and durable settlement should be achieved between Iran and Iraq,

Recalling the provisions of the Charter of the United Nations, and in particular the obligation of all Member States to settle their international disputes by peaceful means in such a manner that international peace and security and justice are not endangered,

Determining that there exists a breach of the peace as regards the conflict between Iran and Iraq,

Acting under Articles 39 and 40 of the Charter,

1. *Demands* that, as a first step towards a negotiated settlement, the Islamic Republic of Iran and Iraq observe an immediate cease-fire, discontinue all military actions on land, at sea and in the air, and withdraw all forces to the internationally recognized boundaries without delay;

2. *Requests* the Secretary-General to dispatch a team of United Nations observers to verify, confirm and supervise the cease-fire and withdrawal and further requests the Secretary-General to make the necessary arrangements

in consultation with the parties and to submit a report thereon to the Security Council;

3. *Urges* that prisoners of war be released and repatriated without delay after the cessation of active hostilities in accordance with the Third Geneva Convention of 12 August 1949;

4. *Calls upon* Iran and Iraq to co-operate with the Secretary-General in implementing this resolution and in mediation efforts to achieve a comprehensive, just and honourable settlement, acceptable to both sides, of all outstanding issues, in accordance with the principles contained in the Charter of the United Nations;

5. *Calls upon* all other States to exercise the utmost restraint and to refrain from any act which may lead to further escalation and widening of the conflict, and thus to facilitate the implementation of the present resolution;

6. *Requests* the Secretary-General to explore, in consultation with Iran and Iraq, the question of entrusting an impartial body with inquiring into responsibility for the conflict and to report to the Security Council as soon as possible;

7. *Recognizes* the magnitude of the damage inflicted during the conflict and the need for reconstruction efforts, with appropriate international assistance, once the conflict is ended and, in this regard, requests the Secretary-General to assign a team of experts to study the question of reconstruction and to report to the Security Council;

8. *Further requests* the Secretary-General to examine, in consultation with Iran and Iraq and with other States of the region, measures to enhance the security and stability of the region;

9. *Requests* the Secretary-General to keep the Security Council informed on the implementation of this resolution;

10. *Decides* to meet again as necessary to consider further steps to ensure compliance with this resolution.

SOURCE: Report of the Security Council, 16 June 1987–15 June 1988, Official Records of the General Assembly, 43rd Session. Supplement No. 2, A/43/2, pp. 4–5.

Appendix 5 The Geneva Accords and the US Statement on Afghanistan, 14 April 1988

BILATERAL AGREEMENT BETWEEN THE REPUBLIC OF
AFGHANISTAN AND THE ISLAMIC REPUBLIC OF PAKISTAN
ON THE PRINCIPLES OF MUTUAL RELATIONS, IN
PARTICULAR ON NON-INTERFERENCE AND NON-
INTERVENTION

The Republic of Afghanistan and the Islamic Republic of Pakistan, hereinafter referred to as the High Contracting Parties,

Desiring to normalize relations and promote good-neighbourliness and
co-operation as well as to strengthen international peace and security in the
region,

Considering that full observance of the principle of non-interference and
non-intervention in the internal and external affairs of States is of the
greatest importance for the maintenance of international peace and security
and for the fulfilment of the purposes and principles of the Charter of the
United Nations,

Reaffirming the inalienable right of States freely to determine their own
political, economic, cultural and social systems in accordance with the will of
their peoples without outside intervention, interference, subversion, coercion or threat in any form whatsoever,

Mindful of the provisions of the Charter of the United Nations as well as
the resolutions adopted by the United Nations on the principle of non-
interference and non-intervention, in particular the Declaration on Principles
of International Law concerning Friendly Relations and Co-operation among
States in accordance with the Charter of the United Nations, of 24 October
1970, as well as the Declaration on the Inadmissibility of Intervention and
Interference in the Internal Affairs of States, of 9 December 1981,

Have agreed as follows:

Article I Relations between the High Contracting Parties shall be
conducted in strict compliance with the principle of non-interference and
non-intervention by States in the affairs of other States.

Article II For the purpose of implementing the principle of non-
interference and non-intervention each High Contracting Party undertakes
to comply with the following obligations:

(1) to respect the sovereignty, political independence, territorial integrity, national unity, security and non-alignment of the other High Contracting Party, as well as the national identity and cultural heritage of its people;

(2) to respect the sovereign and inalienable right of the other High Contracting Party freely to determine its own political, economic, cultural and social systems, to develop its international relations and to exercise permanent sovereignty over its natural resources, in accordance with the will of its people, and without outside intervention, interference, subversion, coercion or threat in any form whatsoever;

(3) to refrain from the threat or use of force in any form whatsoever so as not to violate the boundaries of each other, to disrupt the political, social or economic order of the other High Contracting Party, to overthrow or change the political system of the other High Contracting Party or its Government, or to cause tension between the High Contracting Parties;

(4) to ensure that its territory is not used in any manner which would violate the sovereignty, political independence, territorial integrity and national unity or disrupt the political, economic and social stability of the other High Contracting Party;

(5) to refrain from armed intervention, subversion, military occupation or any other form of intervention and interference, overt or covert, directed at the other High Contracting Party, or any act of military, political or economic interference in the internal affairs of the other High Contracting Party, including acts of reprisal involving the use of force;

(6) to refrain from any action or attempt in whatever form or under whatever pretext to destabilize or to undermine the stability of the other High Contracting Party or any of its institutions;

(7) to refrain from the promotion, encouragement or support, direct or indirect, of rebellious or secessionist activities against the other High Contracting Party, under any pretext whatsoever, or from any other action which seeks to disrupt the unity or to undermine or subvert the political order of the other High Contracting Party;

(8) to prevent within its territory the training, equipping, financing and recruitment of mercenaries from whatever origin for the purpose of hostile activities against the other High Contracting Party, or the sending of such mercenaries into the territory of the other High Contracting Party and accordingly to deny facilities, including financing for the training, equipping and transit of such mercenaries;

(9) to refrain from making any agreements or arrangements with other States designed to intervene or interfere in the internal and external affairs of the other High Contracting Party;

(10) to abstain from any defamatory campaign, vilification or hostile propaganda for the purpose of intervening or interfering in the internal affairs of the other High Contracting Party;

(11) to prevent any assistance to or use of or tolerance of terrorist groups, saboteurs, or subversive agents against the other High Contracting Party;

(12) to prevent within its territory the presence, harbouring, in camps and bases or otherwise, organizing, training, financing, equipping and

arming of individuals and political, ethnic and any other groups for the purpose of creating subversion, disorder or unrest in the territory of the other High Contracting Party and accordingly also to prevent the use of mass media and the transportation of arms, ammunition and equipment by such individuals and groups;

(13) not to resort to or to allow any other action that could be considered as interference or intervention.

Article III   The present Agreement shall enter into force on 15 May 1988.

Article IV   Any steps that may be required in order to enable the High Contracting Parties to comply with the provisions of Article II of this Agreement shall be completed by the date on which this Agreement enters into force.

Article V This Agreement is drawn up in the English, Pashtu and Urdu languages, all texts being equally authentic. In case of any divergence of interpretation, the English text shall prevail.

Done in five original copies at Geneva this fourteenth day of April 1988.

(Signed by Afghanistan and Pakistan)

DECLARATION ON INTERNATIONAL GUARANTEES

The Governments of the Union of Soviet Socialist Republics and of the United States of America,

Expressing support that the Republic of Afghanistan and the Islamic Republic of Pakistan have concluded a negotiated political settlement designed to normalize relations and promote good-neighbourliness between the two countries as well as to strengthen international peace and security in the region;

Wishing in turn to contribute to the achievement of the objectives that the Republic of Afghanistan and the Islamic Republic of Pakistan have set themselves, and with a view to ensuring respect for their sovereignty, independence, territorial integrity and non-alignment;

Undertake to invariably refrain from any form of interference and intervention in the internal affairs of the Republic of Afghanistan and the Islamic Republic of Pakistan and to respect the commitments contained in the bilateral Agreement between the Republic of Afghanistan and the Islamic Republic of Pakistan on the Principles of Mutual Relations, in particular on Non-Interference and Non-Intervention;

Urge all States to act likewise.

The present Declaration shall enter into force on 15 May 1988.

Done at Geneva, this fourteenth day of April 1988 in five original copies, each in the English and Russian languages, both texts being equally authentic.

(Signed by the USSR and the United States)

BILATERAL AGREEMENT BETWEEN THE REPUBLIC OF AFGHANISTAN AND THE ISLAMIC REPUBLIC OF PAKISTAN ON THE VOLUNTARY RETURN OF REFUGEES

The Republic of Afghanistan and the Islamic Republic of Pakistan, hereinafter referred to as the High Contracting Parties,

Desiring to normalize relations and promote good-neighbourliness and co-operation as well as to strengthen international peace and security in the region,

Convinced that voluntary and unimpeded repatriation constitutes the most appropriate solution for the problem of Afghan refugees present in the Islamic Republic of Pakistan and having ascertained that the arrangements for the return of the Afghan refugees are satisfactory to them,

Have agreed as follows:

Article I   All Afghan refugees temporarily present in the territory of the Islamic Republic of Pakistan shall be given the opportunity to return voluntarily to their homeland in accordance with the arrangements and conditions set out in the present Agreement.

Article II   The Government of the Republic of Afghanistan shall take all necessary measures to ensure the following conditions for the voluntary return of Afghan refugees to their homeland:

(a) All refugees shall be allowed to return in freedom to their homeland;

(b) All returnees shall enjoy the free choice of domicile and freedom of movement within the Republic of Afghanistan;

(c) All returnees shall enjoy the right to work, to adequate living conditions and to share in the welfare of the State;

(d) All returnees shall enjoy the right to participate on an equal basis in the civic affairs of the Republic of Afghanistan. They shall be ensured equal benefits from the solution of the land question on the basis of the Land and Water Reform;

(e) All returnees shall enjoy the same rights and privileges, including freedom of religion, and have the same obligations and responsibilities as any other citizens of the Republic of Afghanistan without discrimination.

The Government of the Republic of Afghanistan undertakes to implement these measures and to provide, within its possibilities, all necessary assistance in the process of repatriation.

Article III   The Government of the Islamic Republic of Pakistan shall facilitate the voluntary, orderly and peaceful repatriation of all Afghan refugees staying within its territory and undertakes to provide, within its possibilities, all necessary assistance in the process of repatriation.

Article IV   For the purpose of organizing, co-ordinating and supervising the operations which should effect the voluntary, orderly and peaceful repatriation of Afghan refugees, there shall be set up mixed commissions in accordance with the established international practice. For the performance of their functions the members of the commissions and their staff shall be accorded the necessary facilities, and have access to the relevant areas within the territories of the High Contracting Parties.

Article V   With a view to the orderly movement of the returnees, the commissions shall determine frontier crossing points and establish necessary transit centres. They shall also establish all other modalities for the phased return of refugees, including registration and communication to the country of return of the names of refugees who express the wish to return.

Article VI   At the request of the Governments concerned, the United Nations High Commissioner for Refugees will co-operate and provide assistance in the process of voluntary repatriation of refugees in accordance with the present Agreement. Special agreements may be concluded for this purpose between UNHCR and the High Contracting Parties.

Article VII   The present Agreement shall enter into force on 15 May 1988. At that time the mixed commissions provided in Article IV shall be established and the operations for the voluntary return of refugees under this Agreement shall commence.

The arrangements set out in Articles IV and V above shall remain in effect for a period of eighteen months. After that period the High Contracting Parties shall review the results of the repatriation and, if necessary, consider any further arrangements that may be called for.

Article VIII   This Agreement is drawn up in the English, Pashtu and Urdu languages, all texts being equally authentic. In case of any divergence of interpretation, the English text shall prevail.

Done in five original copies at Geneva this fourteenth day of April 1988.

(Signed by Afghanistan and Pakistan)

AGREEMENT ON THE INTERRELATIONSHIPS FOR THE SETTLEMENT OF THE SITUATION RELATING TO AFGHANISTAN

1   The diplomatic process initiated by the Secretary-General of the United Nations with the support of all Governments concerned and aimed at achieving, through negotiations, a political settlement of the situation relating to Afghanistan has been successfully brought to an end.

2   Having agreed to work towards a comprehensive settlement designed to resolve the various issues involved and to establish a framework for good-neighbourliness and co-operation, the Government of the Republic of Afghanistan and the Government of the Islamic Republic of Pakistan entered into negotiations through the intermediary of the Personal Representative of the Secretary-General at Geneva from 16 to 24 June 1982. Following consultations held by the Personal Representative in Islamabad, Kabul and Teheran from 21 January to 7 February 1983, the negotiations continued at Geneva from 11 to 22 April and from 12 to 24 June 1983. The Personal Representative again visited the area for high-level discussions from 3 to 15 April 1984. It was then agreed to change the format of the negotiations and, in pursuance thereof, proximity talks through the intermediary of the Personal Representative were held at Geneva from 24 to 30 August 1984. Another visit to the area by the Personal Representative from 25 to 31 May 1985 preceded further rounds of proximity talks held at Geneva from 20 to 25 June, from 27 to 30 August and from 16 to 19 December 1985. The Personal Representative paid an additional visit to the area from 8 to 18

March 1986 for consultations. The final round of negotiations began as proximity talks at Geneva on 5 May 1986, was suspended on 23 May 1986, and was resumed from 31 July to 8 August 1986. The Personal Representative visited the area from 20 November to 3 December 1986 for further consultations and the talks at Geneva were resumed again from 25 February to 9 March 1987, and from 7 to 11 September 1987. The Personal Representative again visited the area from 18 January to 9 February 1988 and the talks resumed at Geneva from 2 March to 8 April 1988. The format of the negotiations was changed on 14 April 1988, when the instruments comprising the settlement were finalized, and, accordingly, direct talks were held at that stage. The Government of the Islamic Republic of Iran was kept informed of the progress of the negotiations throughout the diplomatic process.

3   The Government of the Republic of Afghanistan and the Government of the Islamic Republic of Pakistan took part in the negotiations with the expressed conviction that they were acting in accordance with their rights and obligations under the Charter of the United Nations and agreed that the political settlement should be based on the following principles of international law:

The principle that States shall refrain in their international relations from the threat or use of force against the territorial integrity or political independence of any State, or in any other manner inconsistent with the purposes of the United Nations;
The principle that States shall settle their international disputes by peaceful means in such a manner that international peace and security and justice are not endangered;
The duty not to intervene in matters within the domestic jurisdiction of any State, in accordance with the Charter of the United Nations;
The duty of States to co-operate with one another in accordance with the Charter of the United Nations;
The principle of equal rights and self-determination of peoples;
The principle of sovereign equality of States;
The principle that States shall fulfil in good faith the obligations assumed by them in accordance with the Charter of the United Nations.

The two Governments further affirmed the right of the Afghan refugees to return to their homeland in a voluntary and unimpeded manner.

4   The following instruments were concluded on this date as component parts of the political settlement:

A Bilateral Agreement between the Republic of Afghanistan and the Islamic Republic of Pakistan on the Principles of Mutual Relations, in particular on Non-interference and Non-intervention;
A Declaration on International Guarantees by the Union of Soviet Socialist Republics and the United States of America;
A Bilateral Agreement between the Republic of Afghanistan and the Islamic Republic of Pakistan on the Voluntary Return of Refugees;
The present Agreement on the Interrelationships for the Settlement of the Situation Relating to Afghanistan.

5   The Bilateral Agreement on the Principles of Mutual Relations, in

particular on Non-interference and Non-intervention; the Declaration on International Guarantees; the Bilateral Agreement on the Voluntary Return of Refugees; and the present Agreement on the Interrelationships for the Settlement of the Situation Relating to Afghanistan will enter into force on 15 May 1988. In accordance with the time-frame agreed upon between the Union of Soviet Socialist Republics and the Republic of Afghanistan there will be a phased withdrawal of the foreign troops which will start on the date of entry into force mentioned above. One half of the troops will be withdrawn by 15 August 1988 and the withdrawal of all troops will be completed within nine months.

6   The interrelationships in paragraph 5 above have been agreed upon in order to achieve effectively the purpose of the political settlement, namely, that as from 15 May 1988, there will be no interference and intervention in any form in the affairs of the Parties; the international guarantees will be in operation; the voluntary return of the refugees to their homeland will start and be completed within the time frame specified in the agreement on the voluntary return of the refugees; and the phased withdrawal of the foreign troops will start and be completed within the time-frame envisaged in paragraph 5. It is therefore essential that all the obligations deriving from the instruments concluded as component parts of the settlement be strictly fulfilled and that all the steps required to ensure full compliance with all the provisions of the instruments be completed in good faith.

7   To consider alleged violations and to work out prompt and mutually satisfactory solutions to questions that may arise in the implementation of the instruments comprising the settlement representatives of the Republic of Afghanistan and the Islamic Republic of Pakistan shall meet whenever required.

A representative of the Secretary-General of the United Nations shall lend his good offices to the Parties and in that context he will assist in the organization of the meetings and participate in them. He may submit to the Parties for their consideration and approval suggestions and recommendations for prompt, faithful and complete observance of the provisions of the instruments.

In order to enable him to fulfil his tasks, the representative shall be assisted by such personnel under his authority as required. On his own initiative, or at the request of any of the Parties, the personnel shall investigate any possible violations of any of the provisions of the instruments and prepare a report thereon. For that purpose, the representative and his personnel shall receive all the necessary co-operation from the Parties, including all freedom of movement within their respective territories required for effective investigation. Any report submitted by the representative to the two Governments shall be considered in a meeting of the Parties no later than 48 hours after it has been submitted.

The modalities and logistical arrangements for the work of the representative and the personnel under his authority as agreed upon with the Parties are set out in the Memorandum of Understanding which is annexed to and is part of this Agreement.

8   The present instrument will be registered with the Secretary-General of the United Nations. It has been examined by the representatives of the

Parties to the bilateral agreements and of the States-Guarantors, who have signified their consent with its provisions. The representatives of the Parties, being duly authorized thereto by their respective Governments, have affixed their signatures hereunder. The Secretary-General of the United Nations was present.

Done, at Geneva, this fourteenth day of April 1988, in five original copies each in the English, Pashtu, Russian and Urdu languages, all being equally authentic. In case of any dispute regarding the interpretation the English text shall prevail.

(Signed by Afghanistan and Pakistan)

In witness thereof, the representatives of the States-Guarantors affixed their signatures hereunder:

(Signed by the USSR and the United States)

ANNEX: MEMORANDUM OF UNDERSTANDING

I. Basic Requirements

(a) The Parties will provide full support and co-operation to the Representative of the Secretary-General and to all the personnel assigned to assist him.

(b) The Representative of the Secretary-General and his personnel will be accorded every facility as well as prompt and effective assistance including freedom of movement and communications, accommodation, transportation and other facilities that may be necessary for the performance of their tasks: Afghanistan and Pakistan undertake to grant to the Representative and his staff all the relevant privileges and immunities provided for by the Convention on the Privileges and Immunities of the United Nations.

(c) Afghanistan and Pakistan will be responsible for the safety of the Representative of the Secretary-General and his personnel while operating in their respective countries.

(d) In performing their functions, the Representative of the Secretary-General and his staff will act with complete impartiality. The Representative of the Secretary-General and his personnel must not interfere in the internal affairs of Afghanistan and Pakistan and, in this context, cannot be used to secure advantages for any of the Parties concerned.

II. Mandate

The Mandate for the implementation-assistance arrangements envisaged in paragraph 7 derives from the instruments comprising the settlement. All the staff assigned to the Representative of the Secretary-General will accordingly be carefully briefed on the relevant provisions of the instruments and on the procedures that will be used to ascertain violations thereof.

III. Modus Operandi and Personnel Organization

The Secretary-General will appoint a senior military officer as Deputy to the Representative who will be stationed in the area, as head of two small headquarters units, one in Kabul and the other in Islamabad, each comprising five military officers, drawn from existing United Nations operations, and a small civilian auxiliary staff.

The Deputy to the Representative of the Secretary-General will act on behalf of the Representative and be in contact with the Parties through the Liaison Officer each Party will designate for this purpose.

The two headquarters units will be organized into two Inspection Teams to ascertain on the ground any violation of the instruments comprising the settlement. Whenever considered necessary by the Representative of the Secretary-General or his Deputy, up to 40 additional military officers (some 10 additional Inspection Teams) will be redeployed from existing operations within the shortest possible time (normally around 48 hours).

The nationalities of all the Officers will be determined in consultation with the Parties.

Whenever necessary the Representative of the Secretary-General, who will periodically visit the area for consultations with the Parties and to review the work of his personnel, will also assign to the area members of his own Office and other civilian personnel from the United Nations Secretariat as may be needed. His Deputy will alternate between the two headquarters units and will remain at all times in close communication with him.

IV. Procedure

(a) Inspections conducted at the request of the Parties

(i) A complaint regarding a violation of the instrument of the settlement lodged by any of the Parties should be submitted in writing, in the English language, to the respective headquarters units and should indicate all relevant information and details.

(ii) Upon receipt of a complaint the Deputy to the Representative of the Secretary-General will immediately inform the other Party of the complaint and undertake an investigation by making on-site inspections, gathering testimony and using any other procedure which he may deem necessary for the investigation of the alleged violation. Such inspection will be conducted using headquarters staff as referred to above, unless the Deputy Representative of the Secretary-General considers that additional teams are needed. In that case, the Parties will, under the principle of freedom of movement allow immediate access of the additional personnel to their respective territories.

(iii) Reports on investigations will be prepared in English and submitted by the Deputy Representative of the Secretary-General to the two Governments, on a confidential basis. (A third copy of the Report will be simultaneously transmitted, on a confidential basis, to United Nations Headquarters in New York, exclusively for the information of the Secretary-General and his Representative.) In accordance with paragraph 7 a report on an investigation should be considered in a meeting of the Parties not later than 48 hours after it has been submitted. The Deputy Representative of the Secretary-General will, in the absence of the Representative, lend his good offices to the Parties and in that context he will assist in the organization of the meetings and participate in them. In the context of those meetings the Deputy Representative of the Secretary-General may submit to the Parties for their consideration and approval, suggestions and recommendations for the prompt, faithful and complete observance of the provisions of the instruments. (Such suggestions and recommendations will be, as a matter of course, consulted with, and cleared by, the Representative of the Secretary-General.)

(b) Inspections conducted on the initiative of the Deputy Representative of the Secretary-General
In addition to inspections requested by the Parties, the Deputy Representative of the Secretary-General may carry out on his own initiative and in consultation with the Representative inspections he deems appropriate for the purpose of the implementation of paragraph 7. If it is considered that the conclusions reached in an inspection justify a report to the Parties, the same procedure used in submitting reports in connection with inspections carried out at the request of the Parties will be followed.

Level of Participation in Meetings
As indicated above, the Deputy Representative of the Secretary-General will participate at meetings of the Parties convened for the purpose of considering reports on violations. Should the Parties decide to meet for the purpose outlined in paragraph 7 at a high political level, the Representative of the Secretary-General will personally attend such meetings.

V. Duration

The Deputy to the Representative of the Secretary-General and the other personnel will be established in the area not later than 20 days before the entry into force of the instruments. The arrangements will cease to exist two months after the completion of all time-frames envisaged for the implementation of the instruments.

VI. Financing

The cost of all facilities and services to be provided by the Parties will be borne by the respective Governments. The salaries and travel expenses of the personnel to and from the area, as well as the costs of the local personnel assigned to the headquarters units, will be defrayed by the United Nations.

SOURCE: *UN Chronicle*, June 1988.

U.S. STATEMENT

The United States has agreed to act as a guarantor of the political settlement of the situation relating to Afghanistan. We believe this settlement is a major step forward in restoring peace to Afghanistan, in ending the bloodshed in that unfortunate country, and in enabling millions of Afghan refugees to return to their homes.

In agreeing to act as a guarantor, the United States states the following:

(1) The troop withdrawal obligations set out in paragraphs 5 and 6 of the Instrument on Interrelationships are central to the entire settlement. Compliance with those obligations is essential to achievement of the settlement's purposes, namely, the ending of foreign intervention in Afghanistan and the restoration of the rights of the Afghan people through the exercise of self determination as called for by the United Nations Charter and the United Nations General Assembly resolutions on Afghanistan.

(2) The obligations undertaken by the guarantors are symmetrical. In this regard, the United States has advised the Soviet Union that, if the USSR undertakes, as consistent with its obligations as guarantor, to provide military assistance to parties in Afghanistan, the U.S. retains the right, as consistent with its own obligations as guarantor, likewise effectively to provide such assistance.

(3) By acting as guarantor of the settlement, the United States does not intend to imply in any respect recognition of the present regime in Kabul as the lawful Government of Afghanistan.

Appendix 6 UN Security Council Resolution 435, 29 September 1978

The Security Council,

Recalling its resolutions 385 (1976) of 30 January 1976 and 431 (1978) and 432 (1978) of 27 July 1978,

Having considered the report of the Secretary-General submitted pursuant to paragraph 2 of resolution 431 (1978) and his explanatory statement made in the Security Council on 29 September 1978 (S/12869),

Taking note of the relevant communications from the Government of South Africa to the Secretary-General,

Taking note also of the letter dated 8 September 1978 from the President of the South West Africa People's Organization to the Secretary-General,

Reaffirming the legal responsibility of the United Nations over Namibia,

1. *Approves* the report of the Secretary-General on the implementation of the proposal for a settlement of the Namibian situation and his explanatory statement;

2. *Reiterates* that its objective is the withdrawal of South Africa's illegal administration from Namibia and the transfer of power to the people of Namibia with the assistance of the United Nations in accordance with Security Council resolution 385 (1976);

3. *Decides* to establish under its authority a United Nations Transition Assistance Group in accordance with the above-mentioned report of the Secretary-General for a period of up to 12 months in order to assist his Special Representative to carry out the mandate conferred upon him by the Security Council in paragraph 1 of its resolution 431 (1978), namely, to ensure the early independence of Namibia through free elections under the supervision and control of the United Nations;

4. *Welcomes* the preparedness of the South West Africa People's Organization to co-operate in the implementation of the Secretary-General's report, including its expressed readiness to sign and observe the cease-fire provisions as manifested in the letter from its President of 8 September 1978;

5. *Calls upon* South Africa forthwith to co-operate with the Secretary-General in the implementation of the present resolution;

6. *Declares* that all unilateral measures taken by the illegal administration in Namibia in relation to the electoral process, including unilateral registration of voters, or transfer of power, in contravention of resolutions 385 (1976), 431 (1978) and the present resolution, are null and void;

7. *Requests* the Secretary-General to report to the Security Council not later than 23 October 1978 on the implementation of the present resolution.

Adopted at the 2087th meeting by 12 votes to none, with 2 abstentions (Czechoslovakia, Union of Soviet Socialist Republics).

Appendix 7 The Angola/ Namibia Accords, 22 December 1988

AGREEMENT AMONG THE PEOPLE'S REPUBLIC OF ANGOLA, THE REPUBLIC OF CUBA AND THE REPUBLIC OF SOUTH AFRICA

The governments of the People's Republic of Angola, the Republic of Cuba, and the Republic of South Africa, hereinafter designated as "the Parties",

Taking into account the "Principles for a Peaceful Settlement in Southwestern Africa", approved by the Parties on 20 July 1988, and the subsequent negotiations with respect to the implementation of these Principles, each of which is indispensable to a comprehensive settlement,

Considering the acceptance by the Parties of the implementation of United Nations Security Council Resolution 435 (1978), adopted on 29 September 1978, hereinafter designated as "UNSCR 435/78",

Considering the conclusion of the bilateral agreement between the People's Republic of Angola and the Republic of Cuba providing for the redeployment toward the North and the staged and total withdrawal of Cuban troops from the territory of the People's Republic of Angola,

Recognizing the role of the United Nations Security Council in implementing UNSCR 435/78 and in supporting the implementation of the present agreement,

Affirming the sovereignty, sovereign equality, and independence of all states of southwestern Africa,

Affirming the principle of non-interference in the internal affairs of states,

Affirming the principle of abstention from the threat of use of force against the territorial integrity or political independence of states,

Reaffirming the right of the peoples of the southwestern region of Africa to self-determination, independence, and equality of rights, and of the states of southwestern Africa to peace, development, and social progress,

Urging African and international cooperation for the settlement of the problems of the development of the southwestern region of Africa,

Expressing their appreciation for the mediating role of the Government of the United States of America,

Desiring to contribute to the establishment of peace and security in southwestern Africa,

Agree to the provisions set forth below.

(1) The Parties shall immediately request the Secretary-General of the

156

United Nations to seek authority from the Security Council to commence implementation of UNSCR 435/78 on 1 April 1989.

(2) All military forces of the Republic of South Africa shall depart Namibia in accordance with UNSCR 435/78.

(3) Consistent with the provisions of UNSCR 435/78, the Republic of South Africa and the People's Republic of Angola shall cooperate with the Secretary-General to ensure the independence of Namibia through free and fair elections and shall abstain from any action that could prevent the execution of UNSCR 435/78. The Parties shall respect the territorial integrity and inviolability of borders of Namibia and shall ensure that their territories are not used by any state, organization, or person in connection with acts of war, aggression, or violence against the territorial integrity or inviolability of borders of Namibia or any other action which could prevent the execution of UNSCR 435/78.

(4) The People's Republic of Angola and the Republic of Cuba shall implement the bilateral agreement, signed on the date of signature of this agreement, providing for the redeployment toward the North and the staged and total withdrawal of Cuban troops from the territory of the People's Republic of Angola, and the arrangements made with the Security Council of the United Nations for the on-site verification of that withdrawal.

(5) Consistent with their obligations under the Charter of the United Nations, the Parties shall refrain from the threat or use of force, and shall ensure that their respective territories are not used by any state, organization, or person in connection with any acts of war, aggression, or violence, against the territorial integrity, inviolability of borders, or independence of any state of southwestern Africa.

(6) The Parties shall respect the principle of non-interference in the internal affairs of the states of southwestern Africa.

(7) The Parties shall comply in good faith with all obligations undertaken in this agreement and shall resolve through negotiation and in a spirit of cooperation any disputes with respect to the interpretation or implementation thereof.

(8) This agreement shall enter into force upon signature.

Signed at New York in triplicate in the Portuguese, Spanish and English languages, each language being equally authentic, this 22nd day of December 1988.

FOR THE PEOPLE'S REPUBLIC OF ANGOLA:	FOR THE REPUBLIC OF CUBA:	FOR THE REPUBLIC OF SOUTH AFRICA:
Afonso van Dunem M'Binda	Isidoro Malmierca Peoli	Roelof F. Botha

SOURCE: UN Security Council Doc. S/20346.

AGREEMENT BETWEEN THE GOVERNMENT OF THE
REPUBLIC OF CUBA AND THE GOVERNMENT OF THE
PEOPLE'S REPUBLIC OF ANGOLA FOR THE CONCLUSION
OF THE INTERNATIONALIST MISSION OF THE CUBAN
MILITARY CONTINGENT

The Government of the Republic of Cuba and the Government of the
People's Republic of Angola, hereinafter referred to as "the Parties",

Considering
That on 1 April the implementation of United Nations Security Council
resolution 435 (1978) on the independence of Namibia will commence,

That the question of the independence of Namibia and the safeguarding of
the sovereignty, independence and territorial integrity of the People's
Republic of Angola are closely interlinked and closely linked to peace and
security in the southwestern region of Africa.

That, on the same date as the present Agreement, a tripartite agreement
between the Government of the Republic of Cuba, the Government of the
People's Republic of Angola and the Government of the Republic of South
Africa, containing the essential elements for the achievement of peace in the
southwestern region of Africa, is to be signed,

That, with the acceptance of and strict compliance with the aforemen-
tioned, the causes that gave rise to the request made by the Government of
the People's Republic of Angola, in legitimate exercise of its right under
Article 51 of the United Nations Charter, for the dispatch to Angolan
territory of a Cuban internationalist military contingent to ensure, together
with FAPLA, its territorial integrity and its sovereignty in the face of the
invasion and occupation of a part of its territory.

Taking into account
The agreements signed between the Governments of the Republic of Cuba
and the People's Republic of Angola on 4 February 1982 and 19 March 1984,
the platform of the Government of the People's Republic of Angola
approved in November 1984 and the Brazzaville Protocol signed by the
Governments of the Republic of Cuba, the People's Republic of Angola and
the Republic of South Africa on 13 December 1988,

Now therefore hold it to be established
That the conditions have been created which permit the commencement of
the return to its homeland of the Cuban military contingent now present in
Angolan territory, which has successfully fulfilled its internationalist mission,

And accordingly agree as follows:

Article 1

The redeployment to the fifteenth and thirteenth parallels and the phased
and total withdrawal to Cuba of the 50,000-man contingent of Cuban troops
dispatched to the People's Republic of Angola shall commence, in accordance with the pace and time-limits established in the annexed timetable,

which shall form an integral part of this Agreement. The total withdrawal shall be concluded on 1 July 1991.

Article 2

The Governments of the People's Republic of Angola and the Republic of Cuba reserve the right to modify or alter their obligations arising out of article 1 of this Agreement in the event that flagrant violations of the tripartite agreement are verified.

Article 3

Both Parties, through the Secretary-General of the United Nations, request the Security Council to carry out verification of the redeployment and the phased and total withdrawal of the Cuban troops from the territory of the People's Republic of Angola, and to that end the corresponding protocol shall be agreed upon.

Article 4

This Agreement shall enter into force upon the signature of the tripartite agreement between the Governments of the Republic of Cuba, the People's Republic of Angola and the Republic of South Africa.

DONE on 22 December 1988 at United Nations Headquarters, in duplicate in the Spanish and Portuguese languages, both texts being equally authentic.

FOR THE GOVERNMENT OF THE
REPUBLIC OF CUBA
(*Signed*) Isidoro Malmierca Peoli

FOR THE GOVERNMENT OF THE
PEOPLE'S REPUBLIC OF ANGOLA
(*Signed*) Afonso Van Dunem
(Mbinda)

APPENDIX
TIMETABLE ANNEXED TO THE AGREEMENT BETWEEN THE GOVERNMENT OF THE REPUBLIC OF CUBA AND THE GOVERNMENT OF THE PEOPLE'S REPUBLIC OF ANGOLA ON THE CONCLUSION OF THE INTERNATIONALIST MISSION OF THE CUBAN MILITARY CONTINGENT

In compliance with Article 1 of the Agreement between the Governments of the Republic of Cuba and the People's Republic of Angola on the conclusion of the internationalist mission of the Cuban military contingent now present in Angolan territory, both Parties establish the following timetable for withdrawal:

Time-Limits:

By 1 April 1989
(day of the commencement of the implementation
of resolution 435 (1978)   3,000 troops

Total duration of the timetable starting from
1 April 1989   27 months

Redeployment northwards:
  To the 15th parallel   by 1 August 1989
  To the 13th parallel   by 31 October 1989

Total troops to be withdrawn:
  By 1 November 1989   25,000 (50 per cent)
  By 1 April 1990   33,000 (66 per cent)
  By 1 October 1990   38,000 (76 per cent)
  By 1 July 1991   50,000 (100 per cent)

Taking as a basis a Cuban force of 50,000 troops.

SOURCE: UN Security Council Doc. S/20345. [There is a very full collection of documents on the Angola/Namibia negotiations in *International Legal Materials*, vol. 28, no. 4, July 1989, pp. 944–1017.]

Notes

INTRODUCTION

1. However, Switzerland only joined 'on the express understanding that if ever the League were compelled to use coercion against a State guilty of aggression, she should not be expected either to participate in any military action, or to allow the passage of troops across her territory; but that she would take her full part in the economic and financial sanctions which the Covenant in such a case made obligatory for all Members,' F. P. Walters, *A History of the League of Nations* (Oxford: Oxford University Press, 1952), p. 92.
2. *International Herald Tribune*, 11 Mar. 1986.
3. *Financial Times*, 11 Mar. 1986.
4. The case for membership is succinctly summed up by Franz E. Mulheim (Head of UN section of Swiss Department of Foreign Affairs) in *International Herald Tribune*, 14 Mar. 1986.
5. *Guardian*, 15 Mar. 1986.
6. The turn-out in the referendum was 50.2 per cent. Of those who voted, 75.7 per cent (1 591 428) were against UN membership. The rural Appenzell returned 89.3 per cent against. The figure for Zurich was 71.3 per cent.
7. This is the phrase of Leonhard Neidhart, quoted in *Financial Times*, 28 Apr. 1986.
8. *Financial Times*, 18 Mar. 1986.
9. 'Tackling the Real Roots of War', *The Times*, 8 Dec. 1987.

1 THE SECURITY COUNCIL AND SECRET DIPLOMACY

1. Sydney D. Bailey, *The Procedure of the UN Security Council*, 2nd edn (Oxford: Clarendon Press, 1988), pp. 157–61, and Evan Luard, *The United Nations: How It Works and What It does* (London: Macmillan, 1979), pp. 78–9.
2. Bailey, *The Procedure of the UN Security Council*, pp. 10–11.
3. Ibid., p. 41.
4. Ibid.
5. Ibid., p. 43.
6. Ibid., p. 42. See also F. Y. Chai, *Consultation and consensus in the Security Council* (New York: UNITAR, 1971), pp. 7–9.
7. Hugh Caradon, 'The Security Council as an Instrument for Peace', in Arthur S. Lall (ed.), *Multilateral Negotiation and Mediation: Instruments and Methods* (New York: Pergamon, 1985), p. 5.
8. Davidson Nicol, *The United Nations Security Council: Towards Greater Effectiveness* (New York: UNITAR, 1982), p. 74 and pp. 79–80.
9. Ibid. See also Davidson Nicol, 'The Security Council', in Nicol (ed.),

Paths to Peace: The UN Security Council and Its Presidency (New York: Pergamon, 1981), pp. 14–15.

10. Bailey, *The Procedure of the UN Security Council*, p. 42.
11. Nichol, *The United Nations Security Council*, pp. 74–7.
12. F. Y. Chai, 'A View from the UN Secretariat', in Nicol, *Paths to Peace*, p. 88.
13. Bailey, *The Procedure of the UN Security Council*, p. 139.
14. Andrew Boyd, *Fifteen Men on a Powder Keg: A History of the UN Security Council* (London: Methuen, 1971), pp. 4, 42–3.
15. Bailey, *The Procedure of the UN Security Council*, p. 125.
16. 'Some Observations on the Operation of the Security Council Including the Use of the Veto', in Nicol, *Paths to Peace*, p. 96.
17. I rehearse this familiar case in *International Politics: States, Power, and Conflict since 1945* (New York: St. Martin's Press, and Brighton: Harvester/Wheatsheaf, 1987) p. 166.
18. Boyd, *Fifteen Men on a Powder Keg*, chap. 6. See also Hugh Caradon, 'The Security Council as an Instrument for Peace', in Arthur S. Lall (ed.), *Multilateral Negotiation and Mediation: Instruments and Methods* (New York: Pergamon, 1985), pp. 9–13. And on this and other crises, Arthur J. Goldberg, 'The Importance of Private Negotiations', in Nicol, *Paths to Peace*.
19. William F. Buckley Jr., *United Nations Journal* (New York: Putnam, 1974, and London: Joseph, 1975), chap. 14.
20. Bailey, *The Procedure of the UN Security Council* (Oxford: Clarendon Press, 1975), p. 123.
21. Nicol, 'The Security Council', p. 15, and Nicol, *The United Nations Security Council*, p. 79.
22. Bailey, *The Procedure of the UN Security Council*, p. 42.
23. Nicol, *The United Nations Security Council*, pp. 71–2.
24. Brian Urquhart, *A Life in Peace and War* (New York: Harper & Row; and London: Weidenfeld & Nicolson, 1987), p. 228.
25. Ibid. p. 282.
26. For example, Kurt Waldheim, *Building the Future Order: The Search for Peace in an Interdependent World*, ed. by Robert L. Schiffer (New York: Free Press, and London: Collier-Macmillan, 1980), pp. 232–3 (Address at the University of Denver, 25 Jan. 1976), and Report of the Secretary-General on the Work of the Organization, Sept. 1979, *Yearbook of the United Nations 1979*.
27. Report of the Secretary-General on the Work of the Organization, Sept. 1979.
28. Boyd, *Fifteen Men on a Powder Keg*, p. 220.
29. Brian Urquhart, 'International Peace and Security: Thoughts on the Twentieth Anniversary of Dag Hammarskjold's Death', *Foreign Affairs*, vol. 60, no. 1, Fall 1981, pp. 14–15.
30. Urquhart, *A Life in Peace and War*, p. 348.
31. *Yearbook of the United Nations 1982*, vol. 36, p. 3.
32. Boyd, *Fifteen Men on a Powder Keg*, chap. 6.
33. *The United Nations Security Council*, p. 82.
34. 'Some Observations on the Operation of the Security Council Includ-

ing the Use of the Veto', in Nicol, *Paths to Peace*, p. 95.

35. Report of the Secretary-General on the work of the Organization, *Yearbook of the United Nations 1982*, vol. 36, p. 5.
36. See for example his 'The UN and International Security', in G. R. Berridge and A. Jennings (eds), *Diplomacy at the UN* (London: Macmillan, 1985), pp. 56–7, and 'The United Nations and the National Interests of States', in Adam Roberts and Benedict Kingsbury (eds), *United Nations, Divided World: The UN's Roles in International Relations* (Oxford: Clarendon Press, 1988), pp. 57–9.
37. 'The United Nations and the National Interests of States', p. 59.
38. For general background, see Bailey, *The Procedure of the Security Council*, pp. 35–40; Nicol, *The United Nations Security Council*, pp. 108–11; and Boyd, *Fifteen Men on a Powder Keg*, pp. 364–9.
39. Nicol, *The United Nations Security Council*, p. 109.
40. Max Jakobson (Permanent Representative of Finland), in *UN Monthly Chronicle*, vol. 7, no. 7, July 1970, p. 57.
41. Nicol, *The United Nations Security Council*, p. 109. It is also on this ground that they are supported by Evan Luard: *The United Nations: How It Works and What It Does* (London: Macmillan, 1979), p. 30.
42. *Fifteen Men on a Powder Keg*, p. 369.
43. *UN Monthly Chronicle*, vol. 7, no. 7, July 1970, p. 56.
44. Sir Colin Crowe, in Nicol, *Paths to Peace*, pp. 96–7.
45. Bailey, *The Procedure of the United Nations Security Council*, p. 40.
46. *UN Monthly Chronicle*, vol. 7, no. 7, July 1970, p. 57.

2 THE SECRETARIAT UNDER PÉREZ DE CUÉLLAR

1. Sydney D. Bailey, *The Procedure of the UN Security Council* (Oxford: Clarendon Press, 1988) p. 95.
2. *Financial Times*, 24 May 1988; and *Independent*, 17 June 1989. This is perhaps also connected to the fact that he obliged Mrs Thatcher, 'who had raised the matter a number of times', by appointing another Briton to replace Brian Urquhart on the latter's retirement as Secretariat head of the now prestigious peacekeeping operations. In the event, this was Marrack Goulding, at the time British Ambassador in Angola, Brian Urquhart, *A Life in Peace and War* (New York: Harper & Row, 1987) p. 375.
3. *UN Monthly Chronicle*, Feb. 1982, p. 7.
4. Christopher Thomas, 'Friend to the World's Enemies', *The Times*, 28 July 1988.
5. Urquhart, *A Life in Peace and War*, p. 334.
6. During an academic interlude in the early 1960s, he was Professor of Diplomatic Law at the Academia Diplomatique del Peru and Professor of International Relations at the Academia de Guerra Aerea del Peru. In 1964 he published *Manual de Derecho Diplomatico* (Manual of Diplomatic Law).
7. *Financial Times*, 23 July 1988.
8. Javier Pérez de Cuéllar, 'The Role of the UN Secretary-General', in

Adam Roberts and Benedict Kingsbury (eds), *United Nations, Divided World: The UN's Roles in International Relations* (Oxford: Clarendon Press, 1988), p. 76.

9. Urquhart, *A Life in Peace and War*, p. 348.

10. 'Report of the Secretary-General on the Work of the Organization', *Yearbook of the United Nations 1982*, vol. 76, pp. 3–8.

11. Conor Cruise O'Brien's description, in 'Getting Together for Peace', *The Times*, 3 Aug. 1988.

12. *UN Monthly Chronicle*, Feb. 1982, p. 6.

13. Ibid., Mar. 1982, pp. 11–12.

14. The full text of this interesting address, delivered on 24 Apr. 1985, is reproduced in *UN Chronicle*, vol. 22, no. 5, 1985.

15. Pérez de Cuéllar, 'The Role of the UN Secretary-General', p. 62.

16. *The Times*, 28 July 1988.

17. Thomas M. Franck, *Nation Against Nation: What happened to the U.N. dream and what the U.S. can do about it* (New York and Oxford: Oxford University Press, 1985) p. 114.

18. *The Times*, 31 Mar. and 17 Apr. 1986.

19. Javier Pérez de Cuéllar, 'The Role of the United Nations in World Affairs', *International Affairs* (Moscow), Oct. 1988, pp. 94–5.

20. Frederick Lister, 'Exploiting the Recent Revival of the United Nations', *International Relations*, vol. 9, no. 5, May 1989, p. 428.

21. *Foreign Affairs*, vol. 60, no. 1, Fall 1981.

22. The United States had actually been engaged in small-scale selective withholding of funds since 1980, Franck, *Nation against Nation*, pp. 259–60.

23. Ibid., p. 258.

24. *The Economist*, 20 Sept. 1986.

25. *UN Chronicle*, Aug. 1986, p. 63.

26. Ibid., p. 65.

27. Ibid., pp. 63–5.

28. Ibid., p. 64.

29. Ibid., Feb. 1987, 24, 1, p. 26.

30. Ibid., Mar. 1988, p. 87.

31. Lister, 'Exploiting the Recent Revival of the United Nations', p. 427.

32. The Group's members were: Norway, UK, France, China, Sudan, Argentina, Yugoslavia, India, Singapore, Mexico, Zimbabwe, Cameroon, USSR, Japan, Nigeria, Brazil, USA and Algeria.

33. The Secretariat had grown in size from 1546 in 1946 to 11 423 in 1986. A fifteen per cent cut meant about 1650 job losses.

34. There were currently fifty-seven Under-Secretaries-General and Assistant Secretaries-General.

35. *UN Chronicle*, Nov. 1986, pp. 17–20.

36. On the previous role of the CPC, see Evan Luard, *The United Nations: How It Works And What It Does* (London: Macmillan, 1979), pp. 133–4.

37. Thomas M. Franck, 'Soviet Initiatives: U.S. Responses – New Opportunities for Reviving the United Nations System', *American Journal of International Law*, vol. 83, no. 3, July 1989, p. 533.

38. 22 Dec. 1986.
39. *UN Chronicle*, Feb. 1987, pp. 17–27.
40. See also *Financial Times*, 15 Sept. 1986.

3 THE RUSSIAN EMBRACE

1. Edward C. Luck and Toby Trister Gati, 'Gorbachev, the United Nations, and U.S. Policy', *The Washington Quarterly*, vol. 11, no. 4, Autumn 1988, p. 29.
2. BBC, *Summary of World Broadcasts*, SU/8676/A1, 17 Sept. 1987. A translation of the article – 'Reality and Guarantees for a Secure World' – is also to be found in *International Affairs* (Moscow), Nov. 1989. For the fullest elaboration of Soviet policy, see Vladimir Petrovsky's aide-mémoire addressed to the Secretary-General and distributed as UN Doc. A/43/629, 22 Sept. 1988.
3. Thomas M. Franck, 'Soviet Initiatives: U.S. Responses – New Opportunities for Reviving the United Nations System', *American Journal of International Law*, vol. 38, no. 3, July 1989, p. 535.
4. *International Herald Tribune*, 7 July 1988.
5. *Financial Times*, 15 Oct. 1987.
6. *International Herald Tribune*, 4 Oct. 1988.
7. 'Eastern European States: A new vision . . . glimmers of hope . . .', *UN Chronicle*, Mar. 1988, pp. 24–5.
8. V. Petrovsky, 'Cooperation, not Confrontation: The Results of the 40th Session of the UN General Assembly', *International Affairs* (Moscow), Mar. 1986. See also E. Agayev and A. Kozyrev, 'United Nations and Reality', *International Affairs* (Moscow), Apr. 1988.
9. Luck and Gati, 'Gorbachev, the United Nations, and U.S. Policy', p. 21.
10. Jeanne Vronskaya, *A Biographical Dictionary of the Soviet Union, 1917–1988* (London: Saur, 1989).
11. *International Herald Tribune*, 17 Oct. 1987 and *Financial Times*, 20 Oct. 1987.
12. *International Herald Tribune*, 6 June 1988. See also V. Nikiforov, 'On Personnel Policies', *International Affairs* (Moscow), Oct. 1988, p. 57.
13. *Independent*, 28 Sept. 1988.
14. Mikhail Gorbachev, *Address at the United Nations: New York, December 7, 1988* (Moscow: Novosti, 1988).
15. Rosemary Righter, 'UN's Surprise Supporter', *The Times*, 5 Dec. 1988.
16. John D. Stoessinger, *The United Nations and the Superpowers: China, Russia and America*, 4th edn (New York: Random House, 1977), chap. 1.
17. Ibid., pp. 138–9.
18. The immediate intellectual antecedents of this are clearly visible in Vladimir Petrovsky's 'The UN: An Instrument of Joint Action in the Interests of Peace', *International Affairs* (Moscow), Oct. 1985.

19.	V. Fyodorov, 'The UN Security Council and the Pacific Settlement of International Disputes', ibid., April. 1982.
20.	Ibid.
21.	Hugh Caradon, 'The Security Council as an Instrument for Peace', in Arthur S. Lall (ed.), *Multilateral Negotiation and Mediation: Instruments and Methods* (New York and Oxford: Pergamon Press, 1985). See also V. Fyodorov, 'The United Nations and the Maintenance of International Peace', *International Affairs* (Moscow), Sept. 1983, p. 25.
22.	There is a good discussion of the glaring tensions between Soviet philosophy and the principles of the UN charter in Robert G. Wesson, 'The United Nations in the World Outlook of the Soviet Union and of the United States', in Alvin Z. Rubinstein and George Ginsburgs (eds), *Soviet and American Policies in the United Nations: A Twenty-Five-Year Perspective* (New York: New York University Press, 1971), pp. 30–7. See also Franck, 'Soviet Initiatives: U.S. Responses', pp. 534–5.
23.	Ibid., p. 3. See also Alvin Z. Rubinstein, *Soviet Foreign Policy Since World War II: Imperial and Global* (Boston: Little, Brown, 1981), pp. 192–7.
24.V. Fyodorov, 'The United Nations and the Maintenance of International Peace', pp. 26–7.
25.	Brian Urquhart, *A Life in Peace and War* (New York: Harper & Row; London: Weidenfeld & Nicolson, 1987), p. 326.
26.	For full accounts of the 'new thinking' and the remarkable extent of its departure from previous principles of Soviet foreign policy, see Margo Light, *The Soviet Theory of International Relations* (Brighton: Wheatsheaf, 1988), chap. 10; D. Holloway, 'Gorbachev's New Thinking', *Foreign Affairs*, vol. 68, no. 1; R. Legvold, 'The Revolution in Soviet Foreign Policy', *Foreign Affairs*, vol. 68, no. 1; and Seweryn Bialer, ' "New Thinking" and Soviet Foreign Policy', *Survival*, July/Aug. 1988. For changes in policy towards the Third World, see Francis Fukuyama, 'Patterns of Soviet Third World Policy', *Problems of Communism*, Sept/Oct. 1987.
27.	Mikhail Gorbachev, *Perestroika: New Thinking for Our Country and the World*, new edn (London: Fontana, 1988), p. 140.
28.	BBC, *Summary of World Broadcasts*, SU/8676/A1/1, Sept. 1987.
29.	Mikhail Gorbachev, *Address at the United Nations, New York, December 7, 1988* (Moscow: Novosti Press, 1988), p. 3.
30.	Holloway, 'Gorbachev's New Thinking', pp. 71–2.
31.	*New York Times*, 17 Oct. 1987.
32.	*The Times*, 5 Dec. 1988.
33.	Ibid., 5 Dec. 1988.
34.	*The Economist*, 31 Oct. 1987.
35.	Ibid., 17 Sept. 1988.
36.	For example, Angelo M. Codevilla, 'Is There Still a Soviet Threat?' *Commentary*, vol. 86, no. 5, 1988; and Edward N. Luttwak, 'Gorbachev's Strategy, and Ours', *Commentary*, vol. 88, no. 1, July 1989.
37.	Alain Besançon, 'Gorbachev Without Illusions', ibid., vol. 85, no. 4, Apr. 1988.

38. *Independent*, 9 Dec. 1988.
39. Sir Geoffrey Howe, 'Soviet Foreign Policy under Gorbachev', *The World Today*, vol. 45, no. 13, Mar. 1989.
40. Agayev and Kozyrev, 'United Nations and Reality', p. 27.

4 THE AMERICAN REPRIEVE

1. Robert C. Johansen, 'The Reagan Administration and the U.N.: The Costs of Unilateralism', *World Policy Journal*, vol. 3, 1986, pp. 601–41.
2. On Jeane Kirkpatrick at the UN, see Seymour Maxwell Finger, *American Ambassadors at the UN: People, Politics, and Bureaucracy* (New York and London: Holmes & Meier, 1988), chap. 9; Jeane J. Kirkpatrick, *The Reagan Phenomenon – and Other Speeches on Foreign Policy* (Washington and London: AEI, 1983), Part Three; and Kurt Waldheim, *In the Eye of the Storm* (London: Weidenfeld & Nicolson, 1985), p. 185.
3. Finger, *American Ambassadors at the UN*, p. 229.
4. *The Reagan Phenomenon*, p. 95.
5. Finger, *American Ambassadors at the UN*, pp. 302–3.
6. Written Responses to Questions Submitted by Foreign Publications, Dec. 6, 1985, *Public Papers of the Presidents of the United States. Ronald Reagan. Book II* (Washington: Office of the Federal Register National Archives and Records Administration, 1988), pp. 1468–9. In the same volume, see also pp. 998–9 and 1284–5, and in Book I, pp. 508–9.
7. Kirkpatrick, *The Reagan Phenomenon*, pp. 95–8.
8. Finger, *American Ambassadors at the UN*, p. 314.
9. *The Times*, 4 Mar. 1985.
10. *Financial Times*, 18 Oct. 1988.
11. *European Political Cooperation Documentation Bulletin* (EPC Doc. Bull.), 1986, vol. 2, no. 2, p. 113.
12. Ibid., pp. 121–2.
13. Lester B. Pearson, *The Four Faces of Peace and the International Outlook: Statements selected and edited by Sherleigh G. Pierson* (New York: Dodd, Mead, 1964), Part III.
14. Thomas M. Franck, *Nation against Nation* (New York: Oxford University Press, 1985), p. 256.
15. *EPC Doc. Bull.*, 1986, vol. 2, no. 2, p. 122.
16. *The Times*, 20 Mar. 1986.
17. Ibid., 3 May 1986.
18. Ibid., 12 May 1986.
19. *Australian Foreign Affairs Record*, vol. 57, no. 4, Apr. 1986.
20. *The Times*, 24 Sept. 1986.
21. *The Economist*, 20 Sept. 1986.
22. *Financial Times*, 2 Dec. 1986.
23. This is Thomas M. Franck's phrase, employed in his 'Soviet Initiatives: U.S. Responses – New Opportunities for Reviving the United Nations

System', *American Journal of International Law,* vol. 83, no. 3 July 1989, p. 532.

24. Finger, *American Ambassadors at the UN,* p. 325.
25. *The Times,* 22 Dec. 1986.
26. Finger, *American Ambassadors at the UN,* p. 326.
27. *Financial Times,* 23 Feb. 1987.
28. *The Economist,* 12 Mar. 1988.
29. Finger, *American Ambassadors at the UN,* p. 326.
30. *The Reagan Phenomenon,* p. 215.
31. Finger, *American Ambassadors at the UN,* p. 321.
32. Ibid., pp. 320–1, and *The Economist,* 6 Apr. 1985.
33. *The Economist,* 26 Oct. 1985.

5 THE GULF WAR CEASEFIRE

1. *The Economist,* 23 July 1988.
2. Though the Sunnis dominate Iraq, the country's population is at least half Shi'ite.
3. Nita M. Renfrew, 'Who Started the War?', *Foreign Policy,* no. 66, Spring 1987, p. 99.
4. Ibid., pp. 99–100.
5. Shahram Chubin, 'Reflections on the Gulf War', *Survival,* vol. 28, no. 4, July/Aug. 1986, p. 307. On the 'defensive motives' behind the Iraqi attack, see also Philip A. G. Sabin and Efraim Karsh, 'Escalation in the Iran–Iraq War', *Survival,* May/June 1989, p. 245.
6. Renfrew, 'Who Started the War?', p. 100 and pp. 102–3.
7. Shireen T. Hunter, 'After the Ayatollah', *Foreign Policy,* no. 66, Spring 1987, p. 93.
8. Chubin, 'Reflections on the Gulf War', pp. 309–10.
9. Ibid., p. 310.
10. Ibid., p. 309.
11. Ibid., p. 314.
12. *The Economist,* 23 July 1988.
13. Barry Rubin, 'Drowning in the Gulf', *Foreign Policy,* no. 69, Winter 1987–8, p. 124.
14. Ibid., p. 122.
15. Ibid., p. 122.
16. Gary Sick, 'Iran's Quest for Superpower Status', *Foreign Affairs,* vol. 65, 1986–7, pp. 703–6.
17. Rubin, 'Drowning in the Gulf', p. 120.
18. Sick, 'Iran's Quest for Superpower Status', p. 709. After the Iraqi invasion, Moscow had suspended major arms supplies to its client for over a year, R. P. H. King, *The United Nations and the Iran–Iraq War, 1980–1986* (New York: Ford Foundation, 1987), p. 14.
19. On the difficulties in Soviet–Iranian relations to which these differences led prior to 1987, see Sick, 'Iran's Quest for Superpower Status', pp. 709–10.

20. Shireen T. Hunter, 'After the Ayatollah', *Foreign Policy*, no. 66, Spring 1987, pp. 86–7.
21. Sick, 'Iran's Quest for Superpower Status', pp. 710–11. In August 1987 an agreement was concluded under the terms of which Iranian oil was to be exported via a pipeline through the Soviet Union.
22. *The Economist*, 19 Sept. 1987.
23. Rubin, 'Drowning in the Gulf', p. 132.
24. Brian Urquhart, *A Life in Peace and War* (New York: Harper & Row; London: Weidenfeld & Nicolson, 1987), pp. 324–5.
25. King, *The United Nations and the Iran–Iraq War, 1980–1986*, p. 10.
26. These included the Non-Aligned Movement, Algeria, the PLO, the Islamic Conference Organisation, and – at a much later stage – Syria.
27. King, *The United Nations and the Iran–Iraq War*, p. 13, pp. 15–16, and p. 20.
28. Kurt Waldheim, *In the Eye of the Storm: The Memoirs of Kurt Waldheim* (London: Weidenfeld & Nicolson, 1985), p. 172.
29. Urquhart, *A Life in Peace and War*, pp. 283–4 and 322–4.
30. King, *The United Nations and the Iran–Iraq War*, pp. 16 and 30.
31. Ibid., pp. 30–1.
32. Waldheim, *In the Eye of the Storm*, p. 174.
33. King, *The United Nations and the Iran–Iraq War*, pp. 18–19, 31.
34. Ibid., p. 31.
35. Ibid., p. 33.
36. *UN Monthly Chronicle*, May 1987, p. 12.
37. HCDeb. (House of Commons Debate), Sixth Series, vol. 120, 21 July 1987, cols. 205 and 211. According to the *Financial Times*, 21 July 1987, 'The Security Council resolution is the result of lengthy negotiations that grew out of a proposal made last November by Sir John Thomson, the then British chief delegate to the UN'.
38. *The Economist*, 11 July 1987.
39. House of Commons, Foreign Affairs Committee. Second Report, Current United Kingdom Policy Towards the Iran/Iraq Conflict. Report, together with Proceedings of the Committee, 27 June 1988, p. 33.
40. *The Economist*, 4 July 1987.
41. HCDeb., Sixth Series, vol. 118, 26 June 1987, col. 223.
42. *The Economist*, 25 July 1987.
43. *UN Chronicle*, Nov. 1987, p. 21.
44. Ibid., p. 22.
45. *The Economist*, 22 Aug. 1987.
46. *Financial Times*, 12 Aug. 1987.
47. Ibid., 13 Aug. 1987.
48. Ibid., 27 Aug. 1987.
49. Ibid., 5 Sept. 1987.
50. Ibid., 4 Sept. 1987.
51. Ibid., 2 Sept. 1987.
52. Ibid., 14 Sept. 1987.
53. *UN Chronicle*, Nov. 1987, p. 16.
54. *The Economist*, 26 Sept. 1987; *Financial Times*, 18 Sept. 1987.

55. *The Economist*, 26 Sept. 1987.
56. Ibid.
57. HCDeb., Sixth Series, vol. 120, 21 Oct. 1987, col. 723, and *UN Chronicle*, Nov. 1987, p. 17.
58. HCDeb., Sixth Series, vol. 122, 18 Nov. 1987, col. 1058; and *Financial Times*, 30 Nov., 17 and 23 Dec. 1987.
59. Eloquent of this sentiment was the comment of British Foreign Office minister, David Mellor, in the House of Commons: 'The nearer one gets to New York and the headquarters of the UN, the nearer one gets to a recognition that it is merely a piece of escapism to think that a UN naval force is a credible option in today's circumstances', HCDeb., Sixth Series, vol. 131, 18 Apr. 1988, col. 552.
60. House of Commons, Foreign Affairs Committee. Second Report. Current United Kingdom Policy Towards the Iran/Iraq Conflict. Report, together with the Proceedings of the Committee, 27 June 1988, p. 33. See also *Financial Times*, 9 Mar. 1988.
61. *Financial Times*, 19 July 1988.
62. *The Economist*, 23 July 1988.
63. *Independent*, 9 Aug. 1988.
64. *UN Chronicle*, June 1989, pp. 23–5, and Sept. 1989, p. 21; and *Financial Times*, 6 Jan. 1990.

6 THE AFGHANISTAN ACCORDS

1. For a discussion of the numbers issue, see Rosanne Klass, 'Afghanistan: The Accords', *Foreign Affairs*, Summer 1988, pp. 936–7.
2. Lawrence Lifschultz, 'An Accord in the Offing', *Far Eastern Economic Review*, 9 June, 1983; and Bhabani Sen Gupta, *Afghanistan: Politics, Economics and Society* (London: Pinter, 1986), pp. 141–3.
3. W. Howard Wriggins, 'Pakistan's Search for a Foreign Policy After the Invasion of Afghanistan', *Pacific Affairs*, vol. 57, no. 2, Summer 1984, p. 300.
4. Zbigniew Brzezinski, *Power and Principle: Memoirs of the National Security Adviser, 1977—1981* (London: Weidenfeld & Nicolson, 1983), p. 427.
5. Selig S. Harrison, 'Inside the Afghan Talks', *Foreign Policy*, Fall 1988, p. 31 and p. 32; and Ted Morello, 'A Hiccup at the Brink', *Far Eastern Economic Review*, 9 June 1983.
6. Harrison, 'Inside the Afghan Talks', p. 31.
7. Kurt Waldheim, *In the Eye of the Storm: The Memoirs of Kurt Waldheim* (London: Weidenfeld & Nicolson, 1985), p. 182.
8. Ibid., p. 182.
9. Selig Harrison, 'Cut a Regional Deal', *Foreign Policy*, no. 62, Spring 1986, p. 136. The uniqueness of the UN's acceptance of the credentials of the Karmal regime, despite its obvious 'puppet' status, is emphasised by William Maley: 'The Geneva Accords of April 1988', in Amin Saikal and William Maley (eds), *The Soviet Withdrawal from Afghanistan* (Cambridge: Cambridge University Press, 1989) pp. 13–14.

10. *Financial Times*, 22 Mar. 1988.
11. Waldheim, *In the Eye of the Storm*, pp. 162, 173.
12. Harrison, 'Inside the Afghan Talks', pp. 34, 37.
13. Waldheim, *In the Eye of the Storm*, p. 186.
14. Ibid., p. 182.
15. *UN Chronicle*, June 1988, p. 16.
16. Harrison, 'Inside the Afghan Talks', p. 38.
17. John Fullerton, 'Troublesome Trio', *Far Eastern Economic Review*, 10 Feb. 1983.
18. Harrison, 'Inside the Afghan Talks', p. 38 and *UN Chronicle*, June 1988.
19. *UN Chronicle*, June 1988, p. 16.
20. Harrison, 'Inside the Afghan Talks', p. 38.
21. Harrison, 'Cut a Regional Deal', pp. 136, 183; and 'Inside the Afghan Talks', p. 38.
22. Richard Nations, 'Moscow's Funeral Diplomacy', *Far Eastern Economic Review*, 24 Dec. 1982.
23. Brian Urquhart, *A Life in Peace and War* (London: Weidenfeld & Nicolson, 1987), pp. 355-6.
24. Lifschultz, 'An Accord in the Offing'.
25. Harrison, 'Inside the Afghan Talks', p. 40; and *UN Chronicle*, June 1988.
26. Harrison, 'Cut a Regional Deal', p. 137.
27. Lifschultz, 'An Accord in the Offing'; and Harrison, 'Inside the Afghan Talks', pp. 42–3.
28. Harrison, 'Cut a Regional Deal', p. 138.
29. Harrison, 'Inside the Afghan Talks', p. 46.
30. Ibid., p. 32. See also Morello, 'A Hiccup at the Brink', and Sen Gupta, *Afghanistan*, pp. 143–50.
31. *Far Eastern Economic Review*, 4 Aug. 1983.
32. Harrison, 'Inside the Afghan Talks', pp. 47–9.
33. *UN Chronicle*, vol. 21, no. 7, 1984, p. 26; and June 1988.
34. Harrison, 'Inside the Afghan Talks', p. 49.
35. Ibid., p. 49.
36. Ibid., pp. 49–50.
37. Harrison, 'Cut a Regional Deal', pp. 142–3.
38. Nayan Chanda, 'Blood, money and talk', *Far Eastern Economic Review*, 28 Feb. 1985, and Chanda 'No More Evil Empire', *Far Eastern Economic Review*, 18 July 1985.
39. *UN Chronicle*, vol. 22, no. 5, 1985.
40. Harrison, 'Inside the Afghan Talks', pp. 32, 51.
41. Nayan Chanda, 'The Afghan Connection', *Far Eastern Economic Review*, 5 Dec. 1985.
42. Harrison, 'Inside the Afghan Talks', pp. 33, 51–2.
43. Ibid.; and *The Economist*, 21 Dec. 1985. However, on 31 August 1985 *The Economist* reported that 'in the past few months they [the Americans] have become more enthusiastic about the Geneva talks, partly because, according to American intelligence sources, they reckon the chances of the Russians agreeing to a timetable for

withdrawal have improved'. On the December confusion in Washington, see also Rosanne Klass, 'Afghanistan: The Accords', *Foreign Affairs*, Summer 1988, pp. 930–1.

44. Craig M. Karp, 'The War in Afghanistan', *Foreign Affairs*, vol. 64, Summer 1986, p. 1046, and Charles Dunbar, 'Afghanistan in 1987: A Year of Decision?' *Asian Survey*, vol. 28, no. 2, Feb. 1988, p. 154.
45. Chanda, 'The Afghan Connection'; and *UN Chronicle*, Jul/Aug. 1985 and Jan. 1986, p. 13.
46. *UN Chronicle*, Jan. 1986, p. 13.
47. *The Economist*, 21 Dec. 1985.
48. Ibid., 30 Nov. 1985. See also, Alex R. Alexiev, 'Soviet Strategy and the Mujahidin', *Orbis*, vol. 29, no. 1, Spring 1985; and Karp, 'The War in Afghanistan'.
49. Ali T. Sheikh, 'The New Political Thinking: Gorbachev's Policy Toward Afghanistan and Pakistan', *Asian Survey*, vol. 35, no. 11, Nov. 1988, pp. 1173–5.
50. Harrison, 'Inside the Afghan Talks', p. 52.
51. Sheikh, 'The New Political Thinking', p. 1180.
52. *Independent*, 22 July 1989.
53. *UN Chronicle*, June 1988, p. 17.
54. Harrison, 'Inside the Afghan Talks', p. 52 and Karp, 'The War in Afghanistan', p. 1046.
55. Harrison, 'Inside the Afghan Talks', p. 53.
56. Ibid., p. 53; and *UN Chronicle*, June 1988, p. 17.
57. Dunbar, 'Afghanistan in 1987', pp. 150, 153.
58. Sheikh, 'The New Political Thinking', p. 1181.
59. Dunbar, 'Afghanistan in 1987', pp. 151–2.
60. *Independent*, 22 July 1989; and Klass, 'Afghanistan: The Accords', pp. 931–2.
61. *Independent*, 22 July 1989.
62. Harrison, 'Inside the Afghan Talks', p. 54.
63. Ibid., p. 54.
64. Ibid.; and Dunbar, 'Afghanistan in 1987', p. 155.
65. Dunbar, 'Afghanistan in 1987', p. 154, note 10.
66. *The Economist*'s description of Cordovez, 30 Nov. 1985.
67. Harrison, 'Inside the Afghan Talks', p. 55.
68. Ibid.
69. Ibid., pp. 57–9; and Klass, 'Afghanistan: The Accords', pp. 924, 935. On the face of it, the American reservation on continuing aid to the *mujahidin* contradicted its undertaking in the 'Declaration on International Guarantees' to 'refrain from any form of interference and intervention in the internal affairs of the Republic of Afghanistan'. It got round this by maintaining that Soviet support for Najibullah was 'intervention' in Afghanistan, and that if Moscow were to breach its own pledge as a 'guarantor' by continuing this aid after 15 May then Washington was similarly entitled to breach its own pledge by continuing to assist the *mujahidin*; see para. 2 of the 'U.S. Statement', reprinted on p. 154 above.
70. Nayan Chanda, 'Retreating With "Honour"', *Far Eastern Economic Review*, 28 Apr. 1980.

71.   Klass, 'Afghanistan: The Accords', p. 943.
72.   Chanda, 'Retreating With "Honour"'. See also Sophie Quinn-Judge, 'Clearing the Field for the Greater Game', *Far Eastern Economic Review*, 28 Apr. 1988.

7   THE ANGOLA/NAMIBIA SETTLEMENT

1.   In subsequent interviews, South Africa's Foreign Minister, Pik Botha, categorically stated that the December accords signed in New York required South Africa to drop its support for UNITA. See, for example, *Financial Times*, 24 Dec. 1988, and *Financial Mail* (Johannesburg), 20 Jan. 1989. And see Klaus Freiherr von der Ropp, 'Peace Initiatives in South West Africa', *Aussenpolitik*, vol. 40, no. 2, pp. 190, 193.
2.   For example, David Beresford, writing in *Guardian* on 11 Aug. 1988, and Richard Dowden of *Independent* – see subsequent references.
3.   This author pleads guilty to the first charge. See G. R. Berridge, 'Diplomacy and the Angola/Namibia Accords', *International Affairs*, vol. 65, no. 3, Summer 1989.
4.   Fred Bridgland, *Jonas Savimbi: A Key to Africa*, first publ. 1986 (London: Hodder & Stoughton, 1988), p. 292.
5.   *Independent*, 15 Mar. 1988.
6.   *Independent*, 5 May 1988.
7.   *Independent*, 22 Aug. 1988.
8.   1 Jan. 1989. Chester Crocker related that, at a meeting with Fidel Castro in Havana in late March 1989, he had heard the Cuban leader describe the December accords as 'his [Castro's] settlement' – 'On the record' address at Chatham House, London, 25 Apr. 1989.
9.   Senator Clark's Amendment had been passed by Congress a decade earlier (it became law on 9 February 1976) in order to prevent President Ford from involving the United States in war in Africa, so soon after the withdrawal from Vietnam, by supplying weapons to UNITA. Ford and his Secretary of State, Henry Kissinger, claimed that America's hands had been thereby tied by Congress in a vital theatre of the global struggle against communism, while the South Africans, who had been encouraged by Washington (and others) to intervene in the Angolan succession struggle, saw the Clark Amendment as a betrayal and one of several important reasons for withdrawing their forces.
10.   *Independent*, 3 May 1988.
11.   *Independent*, 28 Mar. 1987.
12.   I am grateful to Klaus Ropp for this suggestion.
13.   I am indebted to André du Pisani for drawing my attention to the British role. It is also emphasised by Ropp, who goes so far as to suggest that the Americans, the Russians and the British together formed a 'new contact group': 'Peace Initiatives in South West Africa', p. 186.
14.   The opinion of André du Pisani, reported in the *Guardian*, 11 Aug. 1988.

15. *The Economist* actually argued that Crocker's success demonstrated that impartiality was not a requirement of a mediator, 'The Parsons Theorem, or Is the UN Getting Useful at Last?', 1 Oct. 1988.
16. Simon Barber, 'Creating Realities: Some Final Thoughts from Dr Chester Crocker', *Optima*, vol. 37, no. 2, June 1989, p. 51.
17. Pamela S. Falk in *International Herald Tribune*, 11 Aug. 1988; Jonathan Power, ibid., 20 Aug. 1988; Michael Holman in *Financial Times*, 11 Nov. 1988; and Cleary, 'The Impact of the Independence of Namibia on South Africa', p. 124. This was subsequently denied by Crocker (of course), not very convincingly, Barber, 'Creating realities', p. 52.
18. 'America and South Africa', *The Economist*, 30 Mar. 1985, p. 18.
19. Bridgland, *Jonas Savimbi*, p. 561 and pp. 588–9.
20. Barber, 'Creating Realities', p. 51, and Bridgland, *Jonas Savimbi*, p. 433 and p. 551.
21. Though mediation by President Chissano of Mozambique was apparently employed to bring Angola and South Africa together on this occasion, *The Times*, 12 May 1988.
22. *Independent*, 14 May 1988. According to Victoria Brittain, reporting from Luanda, the choice of the Justice Minister to head the Angolan delegation at these talks was 'a diplomatic demonstration that the four-way talks' were 'much more important to them [the MPLA] than bilateral talks with the South Africans'. She also noted that the official Angolan media played down the Brazzaville talks, describing them (inaccurately) as 'merely between "experts" ', *Guardian*, 16 May 1988.
23. Cleary, 'The Impact of the Independence of Namibia on South Africa', p. 124.
24. Chatham House address.
25. Victoria Brittain emphasises this point in 'Cuba and Southern Africa', *New Left Review*, 172, Nov/Dec. 1988, p. 122.
26. These included membership of the IMF, for which Angola had recently applied but which the United States was currently blocking, *Financial Times*, 2 June 1988.
27. *Independent*, 6 Dec. 1988.
28. This seems to have been considerable. According to *Front File* (London), Dec. 1988, 'There is indisputable evidence that he [Vladillen Vasev, head of the East and Southern African section of the Soviet Foreign Ministry] applied the pressure on the Cubans which forced them to accept the timetable agreement of November 15'.
29. *Financial Times*, 27 June 1988.
30. *Guardian*, 27 June 1988; and *International Herald Tribune*, 28 June 1988.
31. *Financial Times*, 16 Nov. 1988.
32. I discuss linkage in more general terms in 'Diplomacy and the Angola/Namibia Accords', p. 471.
33. Davidson Nichol, 'United States Foreign Policy in Southern Africa: Third World Perspectives', *Journal of Modern African Studies*, 1983, vol. 21, no. 4, pp. 587–603. The various and sustained protests against 'linkage' are summed up with feeling by Chas. W. Freeman Jr in his

'The Angola/Namibia Accords', *Foreign Affairs*, vol. 68, no. 3, Summer 1989. Freeman was principal Deputy Assistant Secretary of State for African Affairs from April 1986 until May 1989.

34. I advance this argument in 'Diplomacy and the Angola/Namibia Accords', pp. 471–3.

35. Brian Urquhart, *A Life in Peace and War* (New York: Harper & Row; London: Weidenfeld & Nicolson, 1987), pp. 317–18, 320–1; also John Seiler, 'South Africa in Namibia: Persistence, Misperception, and Ultimate Failure', *Journal of Modern African Studies*, vol. 20, no. 4, 1982.

36. Margaret P. Karns, 'Ad hoc multilateral diplomacy: the United States, the Contact Group, and Namibia', *International Organization*, vol. 41, no. 1, Winter 1987, p. 114.

37. See the author's 'Diplomacy and the Angola/Namibia Accords', pp. 467–8.

38. Chas. W. Freeman, Jr, 'The Angola/Namibia Accords', *Foreign Affairs*, vol. 68, no. 3, Summer 1989, p. 130. The achievements of the contact group are more fully summed up in Karns, 'Ad Hoc Multilateral Diplomacy', pp. 119–20.

39. For an interesting discussion of these, and the tension between them and the principle of self-determination, see Henry J. Richardson III, 'Constitutive Questions in the Negotiations for Namibian Independence', *American Journal of International Law*, vol. 78, 1984, pp. 107–10.

40. Barber, 'Creating Realities', p. 51.

41. 'The Angola/Namibia Accords', p. 130.

42. S. Neil MacFarlane, 'The Soviet Union and Southern African Security', *Problems of Communism*, vol. 38, nos. 2–3, Mar–June 1989, pp. 80–1.

43. Karns, 'Ad Hoc Multilateral Diplomacy', pp. 101–3. For an insider's view of the formation of the contact group, see David Scott, *Ambassador in Black and White: Thirty Years of Changing Africa* (London: Weidenfeld & Nicolson, 1981), p. 197.

44. For a full and careful dissection of the contact group's relationship with the Security Council, see Richardson, 'Constitutive Questions in the Negotiations for Namibian Independence', pp. 78–88.

45. André du Pisani, *SWA/Namibia: The Politics of Continuity and Change* (Johannesburg: Ball, 1986), p. 356.

46. Karns, 'Ad Hoc Multilateral Diplomacy', pp. 103–4.

47. On the Geneva 'pre-implementation meeting', which was chaired by Brian Urquhart, see Urquhart, *A Life in Peace and War*, chap. 23, and Seiler, 'South Africa in Namibia', pp. 699–702.

48. United Nations Yearbook 1983, pp. 1044–59; and du Pisani, *SWA/Namibia*, pp. 485–6.

49. Thomas M. Franck, 'The Good Offices Function of the UN Secretary-General', in Adam Roberts and Benedict Kingsbury (eds), *United Nations, Divided World: The UN's Roles in International Relations* (Oxford: Clarendon Press, 1988), pp. 85–6.

50. *Independent*, 24 Sept. 1988.

51. 'Remarks to Members of the U.S. delegation and U.S. Officials of the United Nations Secretariat. October 4, 1977', *Public Papers of the Presidents of the United States. Jimmy Carter, 1977. Book II* (Washington: Office of the Federal Register National Archives and Records Service GSA, 1978), pp. 1725–6. This point is also given considerable emphasis by Karns, 'Ad Hoc Multilateral Diplomacy', pp. 98–9.
52. *Ambassador in Black and White*, p. 197.
53. Urquhart, *A Life in Peace and War*, p. 308.
54. Seymour Maxwell Finger, *American Ambassadors at the UN: People, Politics and Bureaucracy* (New York and London: Holmes & Meier, 1988), pp. 282–3.
55. *Southern Africa Record*, no. 51, 1988 (Johannesburg: SA Institute of International Affairs), p. 3.
56. *Granma* (Havana), int. edn, 18 Dec. 1988.
57. *Granma* (Havana), int. edn, 1 Jan. 1989.
58. *Independent*, 23 Dec. 1988.
59. *Yearbook of the United Nations 1982*, vol. 36, pp. 5–6.

8 THE UNFINISHED AGENDA

1. *UN Chronicle*, Sept–Oct. 1981, pp. 35–9.
2. Nayan Chanda, 'Cambodia: Agreement to disagree', *Far Eastern Economic Review*, 24 July 1981.
3. *UN Chronicle*, Sept.–Oct. 1981, p. 37.
4. Ibid., Dec. 1982.
5. *The Economist*, 18 July 1981, p. 45.
6. *UN Chronicle*, Jan. 1986, p. 17.
7. Ibid., Jan. 1986, p. 15.
8. Ibid., Dec. 1988, p. 33.
9. This is Peter Carey's description of the negotiations. See his 'Prospects for Peace in Cambodia', *Far Eastern Economic Review*, 22 December 1988.
10. For accounts of the Paris Conference, see Michael Field, 'Starting to Tango', *Far Eastern Economic Review*, 10 Aug. 1989; 'Back to the Battlefield', *The Economist*, 2 Sept. 1989; and Michael Field, 'No End in Sight', *Far Eastern Economic Review*, 7 Sept. 1989.
11. 'Back to the Battlefield', *The Economist*, 2 Sept. 1989.
12. Robert Delfs, 'A deal takes shape', *Far Eastern Economic Review*, 26 Jan. 1989. Khatharya Um argues that ASEAN itself had accepted linkage at the first Jakarta Informal Meeting in July 1988: 'Cambodia in 1988: The Curved Road to Settlement', *Asian Survey*, 29, 1, Jan. 1989, p. 75.
13. *UN Chronicle*, June 1989, pp. 26–7.
14. Hanoi/Phnom Penh thinking on this is spelled out authoritatively by John Pedler in his 'Cambodia: Danger and Opportunity for the West', *The World Today*, vol. 45, no. 2, Feb. 1989.
15. 'Back to the Battlefield'.
16. Official Records of the General Assembly, 43rd Session. Report of the

Ad Hoc Committee of the International Conference on Kampuchea on Its Activities during 1987–1988, A/CONF.109/13, 30 Aug. 1988.

17. Official Records of the General Assembly, 44th Session. The Situation in Kampuchea. Report of the Secretary-General. A/44/670, 24 Oct. 1989.
18. Official Records of the General Assembly, 43rd Session. The Situation in Kampuchea. Report of the Secretary-General. A/43/730, 21 Oct. 1988; and A/44/670.
19. *Far Eastern Economic Review*, 10 Aug. 1989, p. 11; and A/44/670.
20. *Independent*, 4 Jan. 1990.
21. Ibid., 8 Jan. 1990.
22. Ibid., 15 Jan. 1990.
23. *Financial Times*, 17 Jan. 1990.
24. For detailed background on the Western Sahara conflict, see I. William Zartman, *Ripe for Resolution: Conflict and Intervention in Africa* (New York and Oxford: Oxford University Press, 1985), chap. 2. Endnote 5 contains a useful annotated bibliography.
25. Ibid., pp. 28–9.
26. Tony Hodges, 'Western Sahara: A War of Attrition', in Colin Legum (ed.), *Africa Contemporary Record 1985–1986* (New York and London: Africana, 1987), p. A126.
27. Zartman, *Ripe for Resolution*, pp. 43–5.
28. The following section on Moroccan military strategy rests heavily on Hodges, 'Western Sahara: A War of Attrition'.
29. Ibid., p. A121.
30. Zartman, *Ripe for Resolution*, p. 26.
31. Hodges, 'Western Sahara: A War of Attrition', p. A123.
32. Zartman, *Ripe for Resolution*, pp. 26–7.
33. Ibid., pp. 2–3.
34. Hodges, 'Western Sahara: A War of Attrition', p. A121.
35. Zartman, *Ripe for Resolution*, p. 42.
36. Quoted in Hodges, 'Western Sahara: A War of Attrition', p. A122.
37. Official Records of the General Assembly, 41st Session. Question of Western Sahara. Report of the Secretary-General. A/41/673, 3 Oct. 1986.
38. A/41/673.
39. Official Records of the General Assembly, 42nd Session. Question of Western Sahara. Report of the Secretary-General. A/42/601, 1 Oct. 1987.
40. *UN Chronicle*, September 1988, p. 41.
41. *Financial Times*, 6 June 1988.
42. Ibid., 12 Aug. 1988.
43. *The Times*, 7 Aug. 1988.
44. *Financial Times*, 12 and 31 Aug. 1988, and *UN Chronicle*, Dec. 1988.
45. *Financial Times*, 31 Aug. 1988; and Official Records of the General Assembly, 43rd Session. Question of Western Sahara. Report of the Secretary-General. A/43/680, 5 Oct. 1988.
46. Official Records of the Security Council [Provisional]. S/PV.2826, 20 Sept. 1988.

47.   S/PV.2826.
48.   *Financial Times*, 3 Sept. 1988.
49.   *The Times*, 4 Jan. 1989; *Financial Times*, 31 Dec. 1988 and 4 Jan. 1989.
50.   *Financial Times*, 9 May 1989. See also *UN Chronicle*, June 1989, p. 29.
51.   Official Records of the General Assembly, 44th Session. Question of
      Western Sahara. Report of the Secretary-General. A/44/634, 12 Oct.
      1989.
52.   *Financial Times*, 14 July 1989.
53.   *The Christian Science Monitor* (World Edn Weekly), 20–6 Apr. 1989.
54.   *Independent*, 13 Oct. 1989; *Guardian*, 14 Oct. 1989.
55.   A more detailed but still succinct account of the Cyprus conflict is
      provided in Peter Calvocoressi's *World Politics Since 1945*, 4th edn
      (London and New York: Longman, 1982), pp. 188–95.
56.   An interesting account of the British reaction is provided by James
      Callaghan, Foreign Secretary at the time, in his memoirs: *Time and
      Chance* (London: Collins, 1987), chap. 11. According to Callaghan,
      Britain, with its troops in the sovereign base areas heavily outnum-
      bered by the invading Turks, was unable to offer a credible deterrent
      to Ankara because Washington refused point blank to support such a
      policy.
57.   Ibid., p. 350; and Kurt Waldheim, *In the Eye of the Storm* (London:
      Weidenfeld & Nicolson, 1985), p. 87.
58.   Callaghan, *Time and Chance*, p. 354; Waldheim, *In the Eye of the
      Storm*, pp. 88–91; Brian Urquhart, *A Life in Peace and War* (London:
      Weidenfeld & Nicolson, 1987), p. 258; and Nancy Crawshaw, 'Cyprus:
      a Failure in Western Diplomacy', *The World Today*, Feb. 1984, p. 75.
59.   Urquhart, *A Life in Peace and War*, pp. 200–1.
60.   Waldheim, *In the Eye of the Storm*, pp. 78, 87.
61.   *A Life in Peace and War*, pp. 198, 259.
62.   Waldheim, *In the Eye of the Storm*, p. 92.
63.   Ibid., pp. 91–2. On the 1977 guidelines, see also Urquhart, *A Life in
      Peace and War*, pp. 275–6.
64.   Crawshaw, 'Cyprus: a Failure in Western Diplomacy', p. 73.
65.   Ibid., p. 75.
66.   Robert McDonald, 'Cyprus: the UN Tries Again', *The World Today*,
      Oct. 1984, vol. 40, no. 9, p. 425.
67.   Crawshaw, 'Cyprus: a Failure in Western Diplomacy', p. 74.
68.   Robert McDonald, 'Cyprus: Another Stalemate?' *The World Today*,
      vol. 42, no. 2, Feb. 1986, p. 22; and *UN Chronicle*, Apr. 1986, p. 29.
69.   Thomas M. Franck, 'The Good Offices Function of the UN Secretary-
      General', in Adam Roberts and Benedict Kingsbury (eds), *United
      Nations, Divided World* (Oxford: Clarendon Press, 1988), p. 81.
70.   *UN Chronicle*, Apr. 1986, p. 29.
71.   House of Commons. Foreign Affairs Committee. Third Report.
      Session 1986–87. Cyprus: Report with an Appendix . . . (London:
      HMSO, 1987).
72.   *The Economist*, 21 June 1986, p. 61; and Robert McDonald, 'Cyprus:
      the Gulf Widens', *The World Today*, Nov. 1986, Vol. 42, no. 11,
      p. 184.

73. Nancy Crawshaw, 'A New President for Cyprus', *The World Today*, May 1988, vol. 44, no. 5, pp. 74–5.

74. Ibid., pp. 75–6.

75. *The Economist*, 12 Mar. 1988.

76. *Financial Times*, 6 July 1988.

77. Ibid., 10 June 1988.

78. Ibid., 23 Aug. 1988.

79. Ibid., 10 Aug. 1988.

80. *The Economist*, 21 June 1986.

81. Crawshaw, 'A New President for Cyprus', p. 76.

82. Official Records of the Security Council. Report by the Secretary-General on the United Nations Operation in Cyprus, S/19927, 31 May 1988; and *UN Chronicle*, Sept. 1988, p. 42.

83. *Financial Times*, 25 Aug. 1988.

84. *UN Chronicle*, Dec. 1988, pp. 34–5; and June 1989, p. 28.

85. *Financial Times*, 7 Apr. 1989.

86. *UN Chronicle*, Sept. 1989.

87. These were supposedly secret but appear to have been obtained by the Turkish newspaper, *Hurriyet*. A summary of the main points appeared in *The Times*, 10 July 1989. See also *Daily Telegraph*, 17 July 1989.

88. See Edward F. Feighan, 'Toward a Breakthrough in Cyprus?' *International Herald Tribune*, 9 Aug. 1989.

89. *Financial Times*, 25 July 1989.

90. Ibid., 24 Aug. 1989.

91. *Guardian*, 4 Sept. 1989.

92. *Financial Times*, 5 Dec. 1989.

93. Ibid., 19 Dec. 1989.

94. 'Appendix 4. Cyprus: A Settlement in 2016?' in House of Commons. Foreign Affairs Committee. Cyprus: Report.

95. Among recent works on this see, for example, Conor Cruise O'Brien, *The Siege: The Saga of Israel and Zionism* (London: Paladin, 1988).

96. On this and on earlier UN efforts in the Middle East, see Saadia Touval, *The Peace Brokers: Mediators in the Arab–Israeli Conflict, 1948–1979* (Princeton, NJ: Princeton University Press, 1982).

97. Bernard Reich and Rosemary Holland, 'The United Nations and Israel', in G. R. Berridge and A. Jennings (eds), *Diplomacy at the UN* (London: Macmillan, 1985).

98. On the Nixon period, see Henry Kissinger, *The White House Years* (London: Weidenfeld & Nicolson, and Michael Joseph, 1979), chaps. 10 and 14; and William B. Quandt, *Camp David: Peacemaking and Politics* (Washington: Brookings, 1986), p. 61. On the Reagan period, see William B. Quandt, 'U.S. Policy toward the Arab–Israeli Conflict', in William B. Quandt (ed.), *The Middle East: Ten Years After Camp David* (Washington: Brookings, 1988), pp. 361–3.

99. On Camp David, see Quandt, *Camp David*.

100. Henry Kissinger, *Years of Upheaval* (London: Weidenfeld & Nicolson, and Michael Joseph, 1982), p. 747.

101. Kissinger, *Years of Upheaval*, pp. 757–8. For Kurt Waldheim's account of the Geneva Conference, and in particular of the 'rather peculiar

limitations' imposed on his role by the superpowers, see *In the Eye of the Storm*, pp. 69–77.

102. *Years of Upheaval*, pp. 797–8. For similar interpretations of the diplomatic significance of the Geneva Conference, see Quandt, *Camp David*, p. 36; and Urquhart, *A Life in Peace and War*, pp. 246–7.
103. Quandt, *The Middle East*, pp. 373–7.
104. For a Soviet view, see Evgeni M. Primakov, 'Soviet Policy toward the Arab–Israeli Conflict', in Quandt (ed.), *The Middle East*.
105. *EPC Bulletin*, Docs. 88/036 (8 Feb. 1988) and 88/058 (8 Mar. 1988). See also the statement in the House of Commons by Sir Geoffrey Howe: HCDeb. vol. 118, col. 161, 26 June 1987.
106. Relations between Israel and Eastern Europe also improved dramatically at the end of 1989, *Financial Times*, 9 and 11 Jan. 1990.

CONCLUSION

1. I have developed this theme in ' "Old Diplomacy" in New York', in G. R. Berridge and A. Jennings (eds), *Diplomacy at the UN* (London: Macmillan, 1985).
2. Foreign and Commonwealth Office source.
3. On the conventional distinctions between good offices, conciliation and mediation, see Saadia Touval, *The Peace Brokers: Mediators in the Arab–Israeli Conflict, 1948–1979* (Princeton, NJ: Princeton University Press, 1982), pp. 4–7.
4. Conor Cruise O'Brien and Feliks Topolski [illustrations by], *The United Nations: Sacred Drama* (London: Hutchinson, 1968). See also his following articles: 'U.N. Theatre: Survival Tactics on the World Stage', *The New Republic*, 4 Nov. 1985, pp. 17–19; 'When Nothing is Better Than Nothing', *The Times*, 23 Oct. 1985; and 'Getting Together for Peace', *The Times*, 3 Aug. 1988.
5. *The United Nations: Sacred Drama*, p. 10.
6. Ibid., p. 123.
7. Ibid., p. 66.
8. Ibid., p. 15.
9. O'Brien, 'U.N. Theatre: Survival Tactics on the World Stage'.
10. 'The Role of the United Nations in Maintaining and Improving International Security' (1986 Alastair Buchan Memorial Lecture), *Survival*, vol. 28, no. 5, Sept./Oct. 1986, p. 390.
11. *The United Nations: Sacred Drama*, p. 122.
12. *The Peace Brokers*, p. 16. In I. William Zartman and Saadia Touval, 'International Mediation: Conflict Resolution and Power Politics', *Journal of Social Issues*, vol. 41, no. 2, 1985, pp. 27–45, the strong version of this argument is nominally maintained but in effect abandoned. See also S. Touval and I. William Zartman (eds), *International Mediation in Theory and Practice* (Boulder, Colo.: Westview, 1985).
13. 'The Role of the UN Secretary-General', in Adam Roberts and Benedict Kingsbury (eds), *United Nations, Divided World* (Oxford: Clarendon Press, 1988), pp. 68–9.

14. Touval, *The Peace Brokers*, p. 322.
15. *The Peace Brokers*, p. 321.
16. On the highly distorting impact of the presidential election cycle on American foreign policy, especially towards the Middle East, see William B. Quandt, *Camp David: Peacemaking and Politics* (Washington: Brookings, 1986); and his chapter in his edited work, *The Middle East: Ten Years After Camp David* (Washington: Brookings, 1988). On the episodic involvement of the United States in the interminable Cyprus negotiations, see Brian Urquhart, *A Life in Peace and War* (London: Weidenfeld & Nicolson, 1987), p. 279.
17. Harold Nicolson, *The Evolution of Diplomatic Method* (London: Constable, 1954), pp. 75–6. See also *The Political Testament of Cardinal Richelieu: The Significant Chapters and Supporting Selections*, trsl. by Henry Bertram Hill (Madison: University of Wisconsin Press, 1961), pp. 94–5; and Humphrey Trevelyan, *Diplomatic Channels* (London: Macmillan, 1973), p. 72.
18. Compare with Zartman and Touval, 'International Mediation: Conflict Resolution and Power Politics', p. 40.
19. *The Role of the UN in the Promotion of Peace and Security*. A symposium co-sponsored by the United Nations and The Yomiuri Shimbun, Tokyo, Japan/6–7 September 1988 (New York: UN, 1988), p. 7 (contribution by Marrack Goulding).
20. 'Ripeness and the settlement of international disputes', *Survival*, May/June 1988, pp. 246–7.
21. Touval, *The Peace Brokers*, p. 10; and Zartman and Touval, 'International Mediation: Conflict Resolution and Power Politics', pp. 40–3.
22. 'Strengthening United Nations Diplomacy', in UNITAR, *The United Nations and the Maintenance of International Peace and Security* (Boston: Nijhoff, 1987), p. 170; and Jean M. Stern, 'The UN's Peace Function: International Mediator', unpubl. paper, BISA/ISA Conference, London, Mar–Apr. 1989.
23. Report of the Secretary-General on the Work of the Organization, 1989 (New York: UN, 1989), p. 16.
24. Persuasive suggestions for reform, which are beyond the scope of this book, can be found in Robert C. Johansen, 'The Reagan Administration and the U.N.: The Costs of Unilateralism', *World Policy Journal*, vol. 3, 1986; and Thomas M. Franck, 'The Good Offices Function of the UN Secretary-General', in *United Nations, Divided World*, pp. 91–4; and Franck, 'Soviet Initiatives: U.S. Responses – New Opportunities for Reviving the United Nations System', *American Journal of International Law*, vol. 83, no. 3, July 1989.
25. Official Records. Secretariat. Status of Contribution as at 30 September 1989. ST/ADM/SER.B/320, 4 Oct. 1989.
26. *The United Nations: Sacred Drama*, pp. 76–7.
27. See, for example, A. Yeselson and A. Gaglione, *A Dangerous Place: The United Nations as a Weapon in World Politics* (New York: Grossman, 1974).

Index